THE
THINNEST
THREAD

RETHA J. DORRIS

The Thinnest Thread

Trilogy Christian Publishers A Wholly Owned Subsidiary of Trinity Broadcasting Network

2442 Michelle Drive Tustin, CA 92780

Cover design by: Trilogy

For information about special discounts for bulk purchases, please contact Trilogy Christian Publishing.

Manufactured in the United States of America

10 9 8 7 6 5 4 3 2 1

Library of Congress Cataloging-in-Publication Data is available.

ISBN: 979-8-88738-673-7

E-ISBN: 979-8-88738-674-4

Dedicated to those who believe

TABLE OF CONTENTS

Preface 7

Prologue 17

Chapter One 25

Chapter Two 65

Chapter Three .123

Chapter Four 179

Conclusion 203

Author's Note .207

PREFACE

Why me?

I recently heard a pastor speaking on John 6, the passage where Jesus saw the multitudes of people coming to him, and He said to Philip, "Where shall we buy bread for these people to eat?" The message was entitled, "Did I Ask?" and one point was being made about so many great conversations beginning with a question.

That got me thinking that there are quite a few conversations that begin with a question.

"Hi, how are you doing?" "What did you say?" "Why did you do that?" "When will you be coming home?" "Who was it that called me?"

At this time, to share a few minutes with you, I will begin at the beginning—in Genesis. God's conversation with Adam as He walked into the Garden after the fruit had been eaten began, "Where are you?" Then came another question: "Who told you that you were naked?"

Yet after further investigation, we can also find that the serpent also knew that conversations begin with a question. The one that he poised to Eve: "Did God really say, 'You must not eat from any tree in the Garden'?" (Genesis 3:1, NIV).

Years later, God's conversation with Cain after his offering did not receive the same favor that was bestowed on Abel's offering. "Why are you angry?" "Why is your face downcast?" After the murder of Abel, we find God's questions, "Where is your brother Abel?" "What have you done?"

Moving to the story of Abram's life at the time of the visit to Egypt, Sarai had been taken to the palace because Abram had said that she was his sister. God inflicted Pharoah and his household because he had taken Abram's wife. Summoning Abram, Pharaoh asked, "What have you done to me?"

Hagar, the slave of Sarai who had been given to Abram so that he could father a child, had fled the mistreatment of her mistress and received her own questions from God. "Hagar, slave of Sarai, where have you come from, and where are you going?"

Isaac asked his father, "But where is the lamb for the burnt offering?"

Jacob asked the shepherds, "My brothers, where are you from?" "Do you know Laban, Nahor's grandson?" "Is he well?"

And in the Psalms of David, there are many times that he wanted to start conversations with the Almighty.

"LORD, how many are my foes! How many rise up against me!" (Psalm 3:1, NIV).

"How long will you people turn my glory into shame? How long will you love delusions and seek false gods?" (Psalm 4:2, NIV).

"Why, LORD, do you stand far off? Why do you hide yourself in times of trouble?" (Psalm 10:1, NIV).

> *How long, LORD? Will you forget me forever? How long will you hide your face from me? How long must I wrestle with my thoughts and day after day have sorrow in my heart? How long will my enemy triumph over me?*
>
> **Psalm 13:1–2 (NIV)**

Even Jesus, after His baptism, asked John's disciples, "What do you want?" The disciples, wanting to start their own conversation instead of answering Jesus' question, had one of their own. "Rabbi, where are You staying?"

From *Pride and Prejudice*, *A Tale of Two Cities*, *Alice in Wonderland*, *The Great Gatsby*, and *The Count of Monte Cristo*, we see questions. In *The Strange Case of Dr. Jekyll and Mr. Hyde*, the very first conversation begins with a question. In *Crime and Punishment*, even the young man, when talking to himself, had questions to ask. And in *War and Peace*, there were a lot of questions. And we all know about *Jeopardy*, where the answer must be in the form of a question.

Looking through Scripture, books, ancient history, and even life today, questions persist. Some answers come within moments of the question being asked. Other times we don't get an immediate answer, and we feel like we are in limbo. I could continue, but that is not the point of this writing.

During my younger years of life, I had always wanted to write. From poetry and short stories all the way through to fiction. I had plenty of ideas, began several stories, and even picked out actors that I would enjoy seeing play the characters that I was creating. (I am so sorry, Dean, I waited too long!)

But there was always doubt in my mind; some put there by individuals that I thought knew me and should certainly see that I was capable of accomplishing such an undertaking. And maybe with a little help from them, I could have done it.

Other doubts, well, maybe that was just me. Never thinking that what I needed to say would be of any importance to any other person on the planet. Always believing that my understanding of grammar and the usage of punctuation by no means would be up to the standard of what was required for such a thing as this.

Many years have passed, and life, along with work, has taken up far too much time. A while back, I came across a saying that caught my eye. Usually, when I find a quote, I will put the name along with it. This one does not have a person's name; it might be anonymous. I printed it out and placed it on my desk for months until I got this idea in my head and decided to do it. The quote says, "Imagine the book you would want to read. And then go write it."

Simple, I know!

I typed some of those words on my computer one day, and it brought up a quote from Toni Morrison. She said, "If there's a book that you want to read, but it hasn't been written yet, then you must write it." I guess that is close enough to the one that I have, so I will have to give her credit for this. I must have run across a misquoted version of what Ms. Morrison said.

I sat down day after day, and the words would flow for a while, then that dreaded "writer's block" came along, or I would get sidetracked with other things that were not important. Then, I found a quote from Robin Williams, which helped my mind focus on what needed to be said.

Mr. Williams said, "No matter what people tell you, words and ideas can change the world."

After the recent history that has changed the lives of so many in families of our own and those who are close to us across our country and around the world, I am hoping that the words I have to say will begin to work in the hearts of mankind. Or at least the few that will read them. And by them, may the words spread so that others might realize that, indeed, words can change the world. We just have to be careful of what we say. Sometimes, we don't have to say a word and let our actions speak for us.

I also began thinking that everything that I do now will follow me for the rest of my life.

As far as my opening question, I don't know why. I just want to do it. And at this point, that will have to do.

Plus, I see it as a great conversation starter!

Jewish words translated into English:

Ashur: Assyria

Avraham: Abraham

Bar: son

Bavel: Babylon

Beit-Anyah: Bethany (meaning: house of poverty)

Beit-Tzaidah: Bethsaida

Binyamin: Benjamin

Brakhah: blessing (plural Brakhot)

Cohen: priest (plural Cohanim)

Dammesek: Damascus

Efrayim: Ephraim

Elisheva: Elisabeth

Gadara: Gerasene district (region of the Gerasenes)

the Galil: Galilee

Gavri'el: Gabriel

Ginosar: Gennesaret

Hevel: Abel

Isra'el: Israel

Kalev: Caleb

Karmel: Carmel

Kefa: Peter

K'far-Nachum: Capernaum

Korazin: Chorazin

Koresh: Cyrus

Mashiach: Messiah

M'nasheh: Manasseh

Moshe: Moses

Naftali: Naphtali

Natzeret: Nazareth

N'vukhadretzar: Nebuchadnezzar

Paras: Persia

P'rushim: Pharisees

Rabbi: Teacher

Ramatayim: Arimathea

Rivkah: Rebecca

Shabbat: Sabbath

Sha'ul: Saul

Shim'on: Simon

Sh'khem: Sychar

Shlomo: Solomon

Shomron: Samaria

Sh'va: Sheba

Tirtzah: Tirzah

Tzara'at: leprosy

Tzor: Tyre

Ya'akov: Jacob (also James)

Yafo: Joppa

Yarden: Jordan

Yericho: Jericho

Yerushalayim: Jerusalem

Yeshua: Jesus

Y'hoshua: Joshua

Y'hudah: Judea

Yishai: Jesse

Yitro: Jethro

Yitz'chak: Isaac

Yochanan: John

Yo'ed: Joed

Yosef: Joseph

Zavdai: Zebedee

PROLOGUE

All mortals traverse a certain period of time, some for a short time; others seem to continue way beyond the point of being beneficial. Some might say that I am well past that point in my life. Through all that I have had to endure, sometimes I wonder why I am still here. But one thing that I have learned is what one does with the amount of history they have been allotted is what sets one apart from the rest of the masses.

Mankind walks through the pages of history as an actor might walk across a stage. Some are in the spotlight from the opening to the closing of the curtain. Others are considered extras who might have a line or two in the conversation; still, others just seem to take up space, with no voice to be heard, satisfied to be in the background, to exit stage left and disappear from view as well as from the memory of the spectators.

I, myself, have been shuffling along for more than six decades now, maybe catching the eye of one or two people along the way, but I was mostly content to stay out of the spotlight. My first decade of life was uneventful—a typical childhood as I look back on it. There are a few regrets and thoughts of "what if" that have filled my mind from time to time, but I imagine that everyone has those thoughts at some point in their life.

I am, for the most part, one of the unknown, one of the irrelevant. No great monument was ever built for me; there were not any medals given to me, though that might have been different if I had been able to continue down the first career path that I had chosen to take. Yet, it was not to be. Sorry! I digress. Where was I?

Oh, yes, no medals.

No wonderous discovery was ascribed to me. No one knew my name outside of my family and our small community. I do have the distinction of being mentioned by a famous teacher; however, he never mentioned me by name. Still, that small mention was very memorable.

My parents, Phinah and Maridi, had ancestors come to the region of Y'hudah (Judah) when the land was being resettled. Many times, we have heard the stories that have been passed from one generation to another. The Great King Koresh (Cyrus) had issued an edict that the land should be repopulated by descendants of those who had been taken into captivity from that land. Abba's (father's) family had been part of the military of Paras (Persia), which had been sent to oversee the resettlement in Yerushalayim (Jerusalem) more than five hundred years ago.

Abba's family, further back in time, had come to live in Hazed since the family roots were found to have begun in the tribe of Naftali (Naphtali). Their country had been overrun by the Assyrians, and they had fled first to Dammesek (Damascus). There were some years spent in Harran before ending up spending two decades in Nineveh.

Military service became the way of life for Abba's kin for generations. He often spoke of it as being the most important endeavor a person could do with the days that were given to him. As Abba's forefathers had made their way through military careers, his father's father had plans to make a move out of Yerushalayim westward to follow the dream he had to join the Roman army. He had the aspirations of being a general in what he called "the greatest army in the known world."

Insomuch as our family never made it to Rome, they spent a few seasons on the outskirts of Ramatayim (Arimathea) and then about four years in Antipatris. By the time Phinah was ready to begin his formal training, the family was residing in Sh'khem (Sychar), between the two mountains, where most of the family remained. There he married Maridi, and our family began.

I remember, at a young age, my mother and Abba had a disagreement on how they were going to raise their children. According to my older sister, the disagreement had begun years before but was still brought up every once in a while.

While my mother's family was still actively observing their Jewish beliefs and traditions, Abba had been away so long from his Jewish roots he was more than adamant that we learn the culture of his ancestors, at least that which was more recent. He gave the argument, "Why would the children need to learn of old wives' tales and superstitions? All they have to learn is what is around them.

"We live in Samaria; this is the culture that they need to learn. It doesn't matter if they address me as 'father' or as 'abba' as you have directed them to do; we are part of this country. Whether we walk the roads of this land or the roads of other countries, we will be known as Samaritans."

In turn, my mother could give as good as she could take when it came to what she was going to teach her children. She spoke of us being of Jewish descent, and it didn't matter if we lived in Rome and were labeled as Roman citizens; we would be forever Jews. The fact that we lived in the country of Shomron and were labeled as being from Shomron does not nullify the fact that we were Jews. We might live in a certain country and be known as that country's citizens, but we do not have to lose our family heritage in the meantime. We could still learn what was part of our family for many generations; there was no need to change now.

Abba was not convinced!

While we did hear stories and remembrances of Paras and the greatness of Koresh ruling over all the lands that he had conquered, our main religious upbringing was steeped in Jewish beliefs.

We were able to hear our mother's stories. We would sit as still as we could because mother's voice was so soft. She would begin with stories that she had heard when she was young. Stories of King David and King Shlomo (Solomon); she spoke of Avraham (Abraham) and Yaakov (Jacob), whose name was changed to Isra'el (Israel), which then became the name of our people, of our country. Mother's family, whose roots extended back into history beginning in Karmel (Carmel), had been part of the Jewish community in Yerushalayim when King N'vukhadretzar (Nebuchadnezzar) had broken through the walls of the city and taken the people away into captivity in a strange land.

She did not often speak of the time that they spent away from Y'hudah. A few stories of being alienated among the people of the land and the strong sense of community among the captives kept the small band of believers together. The elders made it a point to tell all the people that just because they were living in the land, they did not have to become part of the land. They had the ability within them to remember the way that they were raised in the Jewish community and not let the laws of the unbelievers dictate how they needed to live.

They believed that they would, one day, be able to return to their land because Adonai had given that land to Avraham and his descendants. They kept their heads down and did the work that was required of them, knowing throughout past history that Adonai would send the help that was needed—in His timing. He would not forsake His people. That belief kept their faith strong through the years in Bavel (Babylon), in Paras, and in the rebuilding of Yerushalayim. Other than stories like these, my mother was silent about all the ancestors had to endure during those times. She said we would hear about it when we were older and able to understand it.

As far back as my memory takes me, every Shabbat, we would observe all the traditions along with Mother. Abba, when he was home, would sit in the background. A couple of times, as I grew older, I would notice a look of confusion on Abba's face as we listened to Mother and responded as we were instructed. I would like to believe that it might have been a look of remembrance of a time in his life long forgotten. But since his more recent family history did not choose to adhere to the followings of the Jewish faith, I realized that was not the case. I often wondered about his thoughts as he watched his family go through Jewish customs.

More often than not, his duties as corporal kept him so long in the evenings that he would remain outside the house in order not to disturb our time of observance. And even though the words were never spoken by my father, I think in his later years, he regretted those many hours that he did not spend with his family.

While growing up, I always enjoyed preparation day more than my sisters did. I would smell the bread baking and see my older sisters with my mother cleaning the house. "Spotless," she would say. "Everything must be spotless." Everything was done in the same manner as she was taught by her mother, who had also been taught by her mother—their tradition.

It was later, when I was well on my way to becoming a man, that I found out the arrangement that had been made between Abba and Mother in regards to the way we were raised, the concessions that were required to keep peace in the family. Abba had agreed to us being educated in the ways of Mother's Jewish heritage. In turn, she was to give up any voicing of opinion as to the marriage arrangements of all her children. Any and all decisions regarding life partners for all her daughters and her only son would fall under Abba's authority.

She was saddened in regard to the situation, crying and pleading to be a part of this particular rite of passage. But Abba just shrugged his shoulders and stated, "That's the way it will be."

And that's the way that it was.

A few months after learning about the decision regarding this situation, when Mother and I were alone, I asked her if she was still saddened about not having a say in the marriage arrangements for her children. She spoke of Abba being the head of the house, and she had promised to obey him in all things, and how marriage was always a bit of give and take. She was aware that Abba would do nothing to harm any of his family and would always do what was in their best interests. You know, all those words of wisdom that mothers pass down to their daughters in order to keep peace in the home (the only reason that I even know this is one day, a few months before, I had slipped into the room where Mother was speaking the same phrases to Remah).

When Mother had finished speaking these words to me, she spoke the words that I had heard many times before. "No matter what we do with our days on earth, Adonai controls all things. No matter what you face, what comes in the future, Adonai knows these things will come your way, and He will give you the strength that you need to do all things to accomplish what He has for you to do."

For years, after hearing this statement, I was comforted knowing that I didn't have to worry about a thing. As I grew older, I began to wonder and question this message. Up to that point in my life, I had been mostly sheltered at home; being the only son, I didn't realize how the world functioned. I was a typical boy, growing up near friends that would visit and play. I had certain chores that I had to finish before the sun went down, and I would join the family in giving brakhot (blessings) to Adonai.

Then, I began to notice how some of the families that lived around us struggled, unable to even afford everyday necessities; I often thought that whoever this Adonai was, who was so kind to my family as to give us the food that we ate and a warm, dry place to sleep, He must not like all the people the same. Otherwise, everyone would have food and shelter as we did. There would be no one who had to be begging on the side of the road, nor would there be those who lay at the gate that led into town because they had no place else to go.

As I matured and began to see things more clearly, I noticed that many times at our meals, Mother would eat very small portions of the food, stating that she wasn't hungry, which in turn kept the rest of the family satisfied. She would continually be repairing rips in her cloak or her dresses while using any extra cloth to make clothing for my sisters. Even though the prestige of being in the military was good as far as standing in society, the wages paid left a lot to be desired. Plus, with four daughters, their dowries had to be supplied.

I remembered then the phrase Mother spoke of Adonai. He controls all things and takes notice of His people. When our ancestors were in Paras and knew that Adonai would care for us, we could know that He would be the mainstay in our lives and would continue on through history to come.

Many were the times in my life I wondered if Adonai was real, if He really cared, or was it indeed, as Abba put it, "old wives' tales and superstition." Yet, at this moment in my life and knowing what I have been through, I realize that Mother was right. Whatever we faced, we would find the strength inside of us to be able to face it all.

My mother had been the one to instill in me the habit of writing down my daily activities and each achievement. She said that in the past, the way to remember was words spoken from father to son, from mother to daughter; an advantage of writing down experiences was a great way that future generations would know of my life. And decades after my life had been completed, the words written down would stand as a remembrance of what had happened in the distant past. My children's children and their children's children would be able to read about life in Sh'khem and the many places that I would travel to as I continued my journey through life. For many years, I thought about what I would write but found that I was too busy with other things and never really bothered to put down the words onto paper. Until now, when most of my life is behind me, and I have nothing to do but remember.

Therefore, this is my writing of days gone by so that others might know and perhaps learn from my life, my accomplishments, my mistakes, my disgrace, and my restoration. While most of what is written are my thoughts and feelings, there will be times when I had such memorable conversations I have included them in order to clarify situations and events as they unfolded over the years.

For future reference, you can call me Gaius.

CHAPTER ONE

My younger years, as mentioned before, were typical. I had three older sisters: Remah, Helgi, and Moreda, and one younger sister, Delai. Delai and I would play every day. Learning and helping around the yard came later when we were old enough to do so while my other sisters helped around the house. I kept watch over a few goats and pulled the weeds out of the garden when needed.

When chores were done, I was allowed to go down the road to Yosef's (Joseph's) house, where he and Ammi, another boy who lived close by, would be waiting to play. Most times, they would come over to our house. I believe that Ammi had taken a liking to my sister Delai. She was a little more than a year younger than me and would stand in the doorway when the friends would arrive. Soon, she would come out into the yard and join the fun.

Yosef and Ammi were my closest friends when we were young. Yosef and his family had lived in the surrounding countryside for generations, whereas Ammi's family was from a country way to the south. They were a little different from anyone else in our circle of friends, but Mother always told us that Adonai did not make all people the same because it was more interesting to learn about those who were not like us. Even Abba made a point of telling all of his children that it was not right to judge people by the way they looked. There is much more to an individual than what someone might be able to see; you have to get to know the person who is on the inside, that one part of us that we like to keep hidden away from others. At the young age that I was at that time, I didn't really understand what they were saying. Ammi was my friend no matter what he looked like to others.

Remah, Helgi, and Moreda were old enough that they were learning to cook, sew, and whatever else they needed to know in order to be a good wife to the husbands that were in their future. They believed themselves to be so mature that they couldn't be bothered with "the children," but every once in a while, Mother would send one of them out to see if everyone was still in one piece. After all, she knew how rough boys could get in their play-ing. I will say that Yosef and Ammi were relentless when we played together, which was part of the reason that I was tough as I have become. Still, when it came to Delai, they were both gentle as they were with their own sisters.

As seasons passed, things changed. Yosef and his family moved further into the northern part of the country. Ammi's parents decid-ed that we weren't the kind of family to keep as friends. After los-ing both friends, I stayed more at home, helping as much as I was able to. There were still boys that would come together to play, and I would join in, but it was never the same type of friendship that I had with Yosef and Ammi.

Over the next few years, I would see Ammi every once in a while, from a distance, and we would wave at each other. We nev-er went against his parents' wishes; therefore, we never met up to have a conversation and find out what was happening in each oth-er's lives. Sometimes, I wish that I had. I believe that I would have enjoyed having a lifelong friend from my childhood, one friend that would remind me of simpler times.

As I grew stronger, I would help move furniture and work more in the garden, tending the plants that Mother grew from year to year. She would always find something that would keep me busy.

Abba also began training with me in the early hours of the day before he went off to the Guard. We began a running regime where he would have me run laps around a section of the neighborhood. As I grew older, there were times when I would actually go with him to the training fields, and while he was doing training with the new recruits, he would have me running laps around the field. He said that he wanted to make sure that I had the training that I would need in order to join the military as he had when he was younger, that the training would enable me to join the Guard and already be able to keep up with the grueling hours of drills that I would be facing. Also, he said that he did not want me spending all of my time in a house full of women; I needed to have some manly influence in order to make me strong and authoritative, which I would need in my future as a husband and a father. Sometimes, I felt that he just wanted to spend more time with his only son, but other times I thought that he knew, with his military standing in the community, all those with any clout would take notice of me.

Every evening, with the exception of Shabbat, with Mother, we would walk down to the well at the edge of town to get water for the next day. The younger children would run around playing; the women would gather in small groups, sometimes in larger ones. Many times, they would enjoy discussing household problems; other times, they would gather to gossip about things that were happening around town.

Boys of my age were busy bringing the water up from the well and distributing it to the vessels that were lined up around us. The girls would try to join the group of women as they talked but were soon shooed away to move empty vessels closer to the well so they might be filled. The stronger boys would then move the filled vessels to carts that sat waiting to be taken to the houses.

As the sun began to set below the horizon, the women would say their goodbyes and gather up the younger children while we, the older ones, would begin trudging up and down the lanes, pulling at the goats that were hitched to the carts to get them to move so that the water vessels could be delivered to the houses. When we were finished at the last house, we would leave the carts beside the houses to await the next evening and another journey to the well. I always looked forward to those walks and times that I had with others whom I could call my friends. We were, I believe, a very close-knit community, but sometimes it felt more like an extended family than just a community. Neighbors were always there to help when needed, and we knew that we could count on each other.

I always thought of our family as being an ordinary one in Sh'khem. We didn't live in the center of town, which was considered the "high society" neighborhood, but neither were we on the outskirts of town. Phinah and Maridi, the military man and his wife, as my parents were known around our neighborhood, were well-liked and included in many social activities, at least in our younger years.

As we grew older, the times that my parents were concerned about social issues entirely disappeared from our lives. I guess they were just too busy trying to keep the family going in the right direction.

There were not any other military men that lived on our end of town. As those with family history so steeped in military service, we constantly heard that many men would be proud to be so high up in the ranks and be sought out for important positions around town. Abba seemed content to be the best that he could be in whatever the military asked of him and left all the rest of the world to everyone around him.

I remember in my younger years, most of my friends wanted to be part of the military. While at play, they would find long sticks and pretend that the sticks were swords which enabled them to stand between the enemy and the neighboring houses, protecting the innocent people of our country. But I had dreams that my future held more than that.

For many years, with Abba active in his service, we would travel around the country. We would take trips to Shomron (Samaria) and to Antipatris. One year, I seem to recall, there was even a trip to Yerushalayim.

I was awestruck when I saw the building in these different towns. I watched builders at work for a few days and was fascinated by the work that went into building such structures. Many of them were just normal houses, but then, as I continued walking around town, I noticed the differences that were evident to anyone who bothered to look closely at the finished works.

And the temple in Yerushalayim was very breathtaking. I heard some elders mentioning the remembrances that had been passed down from generations long ago, how much greater the temple that King Shlomo had built was. With the one standing before me, I tried to imagine something that was more elegant. I could not grasp anything being grander than what I was seeing.

It was in that season of my life that I began thinking of creating a building that would stand out, that people would travel from far away countries to see. When I had spare time, I would draw pictures of buildings that I would like to have built, and then I knew that was what I wanted to do for the remainder of my life.

Some days, I would get out of bed early and sit in the dawning light with my charcoal and canvas. Other times, I would use a stick, drawing in the dirt what I wanted buildings to resemble. I would be so deep in thought that I would not notice Abba had come outside and was watching me. The first few times that happened, he would just grunt and walk down the road. Then, after a while, he would say something about what I was doing and how it would not be practical for such a building to be built. There was no need for anything like that in Sychar, and if I thought that I would go to Rome or any other place like that to build great and magnificent buildings, I was just as much of a dreamer as his forefathers had been so many years ago. Finally, he actually said the words, "Quit wasting your time and do some work that is more productive!" Maybe if I had the courage to stand up to Abba and his desire for me to follow in his footsteps by joining the military, things could have been entirely different.

Sometimes, during those months, I would be sitting and looking over the drawings that I had made of the buildings that I would like to build. I knew that I would do my best in order to accomplish all that I wanted. That was what I dreamed of doing; that's what I needed to do. But in the inner part of me, there was always a thought that maybe the dream was too big. I would never be good enough of a builder. I knew that I could not do it on my own. That's when I got to thinking I really didn't want to be a builder; I just wanted to design the buildings that others could build. Of course, I didn't want to build—I was never good at hammering nails and, even worse, at trying to cut wood.

When I was younger and Yosef, along with his family, still lived in town, I would go over to where his abba and older brothers would be building all types of cabinets. His abba would give us small pieces of wood and allow us to use a saw to see how good we were at following his instructions. Every time I tried to use a saw, it was always crooked. I would draw a line on the wood and put the saw right on that line. By the time I was finished cutting, the edge had left the line. I could never get the saw to go straight, no matter how slowly I would cut. Binyamin (Benjamin), Yosef's older brother, would stop by and look at my cuttings, pat me on the back and tell me that I would probably do better with a little practice—his cuttings always came out that very same way when he was younger. In moments such as those, I thought it would have been nice to have a big brother, one who would encourage you when you were feeling bad about yourself and was willing to help you be better at everything that you tried to accomplish.

Drawing lines for a design is what I could do, and they would be straight as I wanted them to be. Why I could never do that with a saw, I never figured that out.

I could see walls and towers rising on the outside. I could picture the insides with an arched opening separating the room, maybe even a hallway that would separate a family room from another one. That way, if you had to live with your parents, you wouldn't always be underfoot.

I had so many dreams of what I would build—something worthy of a king. Knowing that I needed to start small, I thought of something that I could build for my wife and our family. We could have space so that every child could have a small room of their own. I could think of such things for hours, believing that this could be a possibility for my future endeavors.

After that, reality would set in.

What if I did the designs and those who did the actual buildings saw flaws in my work? Or what if they put up one of my buildings, and a few years later, it collapsed and killed people? Was I willing to face a catastrophe like that? Was I willing to bring shame upon my family just to satisfy a childhood dream?

I began to think that Abba was right; my future would be better served in the military, in a stable work environment. At least it was steady work. There was always a need for military force to be shown, whether it was in town or to protect the town from outsiders. And with all the talk of people around the countryside that was tired of Roman rulers telling us how we had to live and what we had to pay in tribute to Caesar, there was sure to come a time when there would be an uprising against Rome. There seemed to be quite a lot of these people around that wanted to put a stop to this in any way that they could. Being in the military would be the first line of defense that might be needed if those people came into our town.

For a few years, I had a part-time job of a sort, helping out on a couple of farms in the area. I would help sow the grain and would also help during harvest time. If they needed help with other things, all they did was ask, and I would help in any way that I could. Abba had said that even if I didn't go into farm work, at least the experience that I got through the work that I did would help me throughout my family life. I wasn't paid a lot in wages as the farms were small, but what I made, I saved for the life that I would have in the future.

As traditions stood, marriages for my sisters and me had been arranged. My sisters did all right with the men that were chosen for them; at least, that's how it looked from my point of view. They never spoke any differently while in front of our parents or me, so I guessed that they were satisfied. Remah was espoused to a teacher, Helgi to a military man (who became Abba's favorite—I wonder why!), Moreda's husband was from a family of fishermen whose fishing business supplied food for the entire region surrounding K'far-Nachum (Capernaum), and Delai's husband commanded a ship that transported goods from Corinth to Egypt. Each would be taken care of and would raise their children as they had been taught.

For me, well, the good thing is that Giesell and I had grown up knowing each other. Years ago, we met on those evening visits to the well. She would be huddled in a group of girls talking about who knows what, as I was with the boys who, at first, were moving empty vessels closer to the well so that they could be filled with water. As time went by, the older girls began moving the empty vessels while we, older boys, would move the filled ones onto the carts that stood nearby. That is when we first began conversing with each other. And it didn't take long for me to begin to look forward to that time of the day when I could talk to Giesell.

Her family lived down the road from us for about ten years. Abba knew her father, Kelan, had deep ties in the highest level of the city council. He saw our union as a possible step up for him. It might have led to a higher ranking in the military. When the betrothal was announced, Giesell and I began to look forward to the life that was before us.

While we waited for those few months to pass, Abba arranged for my career in the military to begin. I wasn't eager about that at first because, in my heart, I knew that I wanted so much more, something different. But as Abba and his abba before him, I too gave in to what was thought to be the best choice for me.

My mother had a few words to say on the subject. "Gaius is too young," she would put up this argument with Abba every time he would begin talking about taking me down to the registration tent. Maybe she believed that I would become more like Abba than even she could handle. I tried to reassure her on those occasions that I was my own person and would remember my upbringing.

If it were only that simple.

As I began my eighteenth year, Abba said that I had "played around" enough. It was time for me to get serious about my career and become a man that was prepared to support a household. The next morning, he woke me early and had me get dressed in order to take a walk down to headquarters. I was signed up and began training within three hours.

As time went by, after a slow start, I just tried to keep my head down, going through the motions of being a military man. I guess I must have done something right. I was put in charge of a group of trainees. I thought maybe Abba had pulled a few strings in order for me to be put into a position of authority, no matter how small.

One day, I asked him about it. He looked at me in surprise. "Gaius, when have you ever known me to do anything to make your life easier? What would that teach you?"

Well, he had a point.

He brought his hand up, placed it on my shoulder, and looked me in the eye. "Son, my job is not to make things easy for you; my job is to make you aware of what the world expects of you, to get you to the path where you can discover what you will become. What *that* is, I do not know at this time; but I realize that whatever it is, you will find it within yourself to stand up to whatever comes your way."

"Abba, I have seen the men that I am training, and they can do things that I never believed myself possible to do. How am I to be a leader when I cannot lead as others?"

There was a slight grin coming to his face as he answered, "Gaius, it is not that you cannot do the same things any other man can do; it is only that you show them what needs to be done to the best of your ability. You know how things are expected to be done around here, and you do your job. You are to convey that knowledge to those men under your command." He thought for a moment, motioned for me to sit down, and then began again.

"Do you remember when you were younger, and Remah was having an argument with Helgi? It was about some boy across town. He and his family had just moved in from the northern country and had bought land to begin farming. Helgi had been listening to what was being said around town, that this family were only deceivers and none of the family could be trusted. Remah insisted that all of that talk was the result of someone new moving into town; people were afraid of someone different than the neighbors with whom they had spent their lives. They thought of the family as outsiders, ones that would never fit into our community.

"That family struggled for months, trying to get the farm to the point where they could produce a crop. But they continued to fight against the odds, and it finally paid off. The father took all that he had learned from his father and went on to bring the fields to bear the crops needed. That man instilled in his sons and all his children to take what was on the inside of them. They took the knowledge that was passed on from all generations, choosing to do what they were meant to do to the best of their ability and not letting some words that people were saying undermine their character and keep them from accomplishing all that they were capable of doing. Yes, the father was a farmer, and he became a good farmer, but within his children was the potential to do things so much better. Within a few years of moving into our town, they had taken the small farm that they had purchased and built it up so much that it has continued to support our community ever since.

"These children had taken the wisdom and the knowledge that their father had shown them and then taken their abilities to make it even more than their father had even imagined. They have expanded their lands and continued to grow the crops needed, and I understand that they are now able to supply much of the food for many of the surrounding towns in this area.

"One lesson that teaches us is just because someone did not grow up in your neighborhood does not mean that they cannot become part of your community, helping others that cannot help themselves.

"Another lesson that I have tried to show you: we both know what is expected in us, as men, as leaders in our family as well as in the military. Knowing that the best I can do is show you all that I am capable of doing and showing you what I have learned throughout my life. I have only the strength and knowledge that I have. Yes, I can push myself to do more. But I would have to ask myself, is that my best, or am I just trying to outdo someone else?

"That is your job. You are to be 'an abba' for every trainee that comes to be in your group. Every single man that you train will either do exactly as you or they will have the capability to take that training, that knowledge, even further. You are showing what you can do while, at the same time, letting them know that they can do more by using the power that is within them, the strength that will push them on to better things. You don't hold them back by telling them that they can only do the same as you, but it doesn't mean that you are weaker by any means. You do the best that *you* can and push others to succeed in the ways that only they can. Someone might even become a general of the Guard sometime in the future. When they do, it will be a result of what you taught them.

"You also have to remember that not everyone is going to exceed you. That doesn't mean that you have failed. There are those people who don't believe in their abilities. They see others doing so much, and they think so little of themselves that they don't push on. They give up and live their lives, many times as only half a man. When you meet those people, you do your best to let them know that they are capable of doing more. Push them to see that all they need is confidence, and they will find the power to do what they need to do.

"Just remember: while some of us have the vision, others find the solution."

He got to his feet, turned to leave, and then stopped. Looking at me once more, he spoke, "You, Gaius, have so much more inside of you, and you will take what I have taught you, what your mother has taught you, and go further than I have been able to do. What you do with that strength, that knowledge is what will lead you through all that you will be facing next week, next year, and even ten years down the road. We do not know what will be coming, even within the next hours. All that can be accomplished has to come from what we have been taught, and what we have inside of us will give us the strength to do what is necessary to make it through whatever comes our way." With that, he went back to his duties.

As I look back on that day and all the days of my life with Abba, I cannot remember any time that we actually had a conversation as long as that one was. And sometimes, after reflecting on that, it made me sad that Abba and I were never capable of communicating as I think should have been possible between a father and his son. I also wondered if it would be like that between my sons and me.

After that talk, I began to take my duties more seriously. While my supervisors knew all the family members that had recently walked the same steps as me, they soon realized that I could accomplish the same and even more if given the opportunity. It was during that time I figured this might be where I was meant to be. I wanted to continue to be a success in all that I set out to do, and I thought this might be a good beginning.

Still, many nights after that, I wondered what my life would have been if only I had made a different choice in what I was doing with all that had been given to me.

Giesell was so happy that I had been given more responsibilities—she stated that she just knew that one day, I would have a higher rank which, in turn, would bring about more recognition from people in a higher class. I realized, from years of friendship and confidential conversations with her, that it was her dream to have a house on the other side of town, to be welcomed at the big celebrations that came with being in the so-called upper class. She became obsessed with pulling us further up in society than any in her family had ever known. Sometimes, that really bothered me, as I had never been concerned about such matters. Having the knowledge of how her life had been up to that point, I wanted to do all that I could in order to see that twinkle in her eyes continue throughout our life together.

Eight months later, we were married. The first year was filled with wonder as we learned more about each other, making plans for our family and enjoying time in our community.

I know what you have heard—arranged marriages are for convenience, social status, or other such things. That may be the case for most people, but for Giesell and me, our marriage was for love. We knew each other's flaws, strengths, and weaknesses, yet it was like we were two parts of a whole person. Through our marriage, we were complete. So different from the earlier dreams of my life to the place where I found myself at this time in my career, I know deep down in my soul that I was meant to have Giesell as my wife for the rest of my life. She was meant for me!

Giesell became active with the ladies of our neighborhood, always cooking and gardening. We had a few goats and sheep, which her younger brothers, Kalev (Caleb) and Adram, watched along with their family's flock. We had not quite made it to the other side of town, but Giesell hadn't given up on that dream. She realized that no matter how much pull either one of our fathers had, things would have to come by my own merit.

My career with the Guard kept me busy, but the time that I had at home with my beloved Giesell was the best life that I could possibly have dreamed of obtaining. For me, it didn't matter where we lived as long as we were together.

While family and friends kept asking about when we would be expanding our family, no such announcement was forthcoming. Prayer had gone unanswered thus far, but I continued to ask for the favor of Adonai to be upon us. As Mother constantly informed us, we knew when the time was right, it would come to pass.

Then, the unbelievable happened.

For months, we had been aware of an inspection of the Guard, which happens twice a year; yet this time, it seemed to be of more importance than any other time in all my remembrances. According to Abba, he had never seen so much attention being given to any inspection throughout his career with the Guard.

Five dignitaries from Yafo (Joppa) were traveling through the countryside on their way to Beit-Anyah (Bethany), East of the Jordan. They had been invited for the inspection of the Guard. It seems that one of the five was a relative of one of our generals. The talk was that he and his relative had gotten into a heated discussion about whose military strategy was best. After some disagreement, the General of Yafo's Royal Protectorate decided the way to put this to rest was to stop by our regiment and see for himself. In our part of the country, news had spread of the spectacular example of the Guard at Sh'khem, and it was not unusual for visitors to stop by to see how things were run. Many, in turn, would take what they had learned in watching our drills back to their own companies and implement those procedures to make their military better.

The previous four months, after learning of the impending visitation, I had been making preparations for this visit, and things were very tense. The pressure coming from the outside, from my superiors, was beginning to build up great agitation inside of me. I know that I wasn't in the greatest of moods, whether I was at work or at home. I realized that Giesell was very joyful each day when I left the house for my duties. She would have the whole day without some moody, short-tempered guy around the house. I am sure that she was hoping that when I returned every evening, I would be her loving husband once again. Many were the nights that I disappointed her on that matter. As the final days before the inspection approached, I found time one morning to apologize for my behavior.

I explained to her that I had been working so hard because I wanted everything to be perfect. If anything were to go wrong, it would reflect badly, not only on me but on those men who had put me in charge. It was the first time that I would be in charge of such an important inspection. The knowledge that the dignitaries would be within hearing distance of all that I spoke while in front of my men made me sick to my stomach. After those few months that I had been in service, I had finally earned the respect of many of those who held a higher rank than I. The responsibilities that I had were so much more than many of my peers faced each day. And along with the accountability that I felt, the tension was sometimes unbearable. Giesell forgave me, knowing that there would soon be no further reason for me being tense. Things could now return to normal.

At last, the morning of the event dawned. I had been up for a while before the sun began its snail-like pace over the horizon. The weather was perfect; just a couple of clouds speckled the sky, and there was a light breeze coming around the mountains.

Giesell helped me that morning in the preparations leading up to the fanfare that would soon begin. Knowing that I would be scrutinized by everyone in attendance, she made sure that my uniform was cleaned, the buttons glistened in the sun, and my shoes were scuff-free.

As I dressed, Giesell commented on a small red spot on my shoulder, saying that she thought that I had been out in the sun too long without my tunic. Nothing more was said about it, and by the time I left the house, the exchange had slipped my mind. In the days to come, we would both come to remember that moment.

The inspection drills went well. There was great applause at the end, and I felt quite a lot of slaps on my back, along with words of praise for the way we handled it all. When I arrived home to celebrate with Giesell, I was so relieved that the ordeal was behind me. After an evening with my wife, I enjoyed a night's sleep like I had not for about a month.

I guess that it had been about three days after first noticing the red spot I noticed that there was a rash creeping up the side of my neck. Giesell, I could tell, was shaken at the way that it had spread over such a large area.

While I went on with the business of my day, Giesell walked over to speak with her mother to ask advice from her and the elderly women who lived in the neighborhood. Surely, someone must have experienced a similar problem.

I arrived home that evening to find her in tears, pacing around the yard. As she guided me into the house, she began to tell me what she had learned that day. Absolutely nothing! No one in her family nor anyone in the neighborhood had ever seen or heard about anything like this.

I tried to soothe her through the evening meal and finally convinced her to sleep. While she lay there, tossing about, I stood at the door, mulling over in my mind the choices that I had to make.

Even though we still had contact with my family, the usual gathering for big family events and holy day celebrations, my sisters and I were not as close as when we were younger and were all living at home. Most of it was because after they got married, they all moved away, following their husbands and only visited occasionally. I felt a deep loss after Delai left with her new husband. We were so much closer to each other than with our older sisters, as we were closer in age and had more in common.

My mother had not really approved of Abba's choice of Giesell as a bride for me. She had known several eligible girls who had been raised considerably deeper in our faith and would have been a perfect example to any children that we should have in our future. But as far as he was concerned, we were still a Samaritan family, so Abba's choice for a wife for me would be as he decided.

Giesell's family, including her parents, Kelah and Zipha, did not have the same devotion to their Jewish heritage; very seldom did they celebrate any of the holy days and never observed the Shabbat, even though many generations earlier, the family lineage was a prominent part of the tribe of Mnasheh (Manasseh). As time went by, there was more influence of the Assyrian beliefs being practiced by her family along with the cultures under which scores of generations had been brought up during their time in Bavel.

After our marriage took place, I would ask Giesell to be ready early before Shabbat began. I made sure that I was able to leave work in time to go home. Then, she and I would walk over to observe Shabbat with my mother. For the first few months, Giesell would put up a fuss and stated that she wanted to stay in her own home, as was the custom of her family. I told her that we were raised to believe that this was time to spend with family until we had a family of our own. I would much rather be with other family members. And since her family did not observe the Jewish ritual, we would have no need to go to their home.

It was then that she began to pick up details as Mother would say, "Kiddush." A few times, Giesell would be invited over early in the day, and Mother taught her how to bake the challah. During those visits, Mother took the opportunity to speak of the Jewish history of her family along with the heritage of the different tribes as she remembered learning herself. After a couple of months, Giesell just made it a habit of going over early in the morning to help Mother prepare for the evening's celebration. I believe that they were getting to be a little closer in their relationship.

But this night, spending a restless night with very little sleep, I then awakened Giesell and mentioned my plans to her. As she went about making preparations, I walked down to the Guard headquarters and spoke to a couple of my superiors. I requested some time off from my duties. Since I had never before needed time away, they were in agreement that I deserved a few days away from the place. They believed that things could go smoothly for the short time that I would be gone. I returned to the house to find Giesell waiting for me. She had breakfast on the table. As we finished our meal and cleared up the few dishes that had been used, very few words were spoken as each of us was deep in thought of what the coming hours would reveal. We gathered together a few things and started the walk across town to visit with my parents.

I knew that at this time of the day, Abba would not be there. I did realize that when he did not see me on the field with my trainees, he would begin to wonder and ask around to see why I was not at my post.

My mother's surprise was evident when she met us at the door. I guess that this was the first time in about five months that we had made the short trip without announcing our intentions beforehand outside the weekends when we would arrive to partake of Shabbat. She started bustling around the room, readying a meal for us. Giesell explained that we had just finished our morning meal before coming across town. When she heard that, Mother stopped what she was doing, sat down, and waited to hear why we had made the trip. For a couple of seconds, the look on her face told me that she was expecting to hear the news of a baby. But after taking another glance at both of us, noticing the haggard look that I knew was on my face and the tell-tale signs of crying on Giesell's, she quickly realized that wasn't the case. Then she softly spoke, "Is it your abba?"

I quickly assured her that it was not, as I took her hands in mine and apologized for allowing her to think such a thing. As I dropped her hands, I raised mine and pulled the piece of cloth away from my neck, asking her to look and tell me if she could tell us what was wrong with my neck. She rose to her feet and brushed my hair aside, looking closely at my neck. I heard her gasp. When I turned to look at her, I saw a look that I had never seen on the face of my mother.

Through all the years of growing up, with all the typical mischievous nature that all of us boys tend to display, I had come home with my share of skinned knees, scraped elbows, and scratches. A couple of times that I can remember, I showed up with a blackened eye. She would always tend to her wounded son, shake her head and mutter something about the ways of boys she would never understand. Never in all those years had she ever had a terrified look as I saw on her face that day. I looked at her questioningly and heard a word that I never believed possible.

"Tzara'at (leprosy)."

Immediately I felt my knees give way, and I sat down, the blood draining from my face. In my mind, I went back to a time in my childhood.

I guess that it might have been in my fifth year on the day that I was remembering. It was early spring; the days were still cool, but the sun was shining, and the grass was growing. Mother had told

Moreda to take Delai and me down toward town to a neighbor's house for—well, the reason for the trip, I don't remember. It was what happened on our way back home that stuck in my memory. Delai and I were dawdling along behind Moreda, who was in a hurry to get us home so she could be done with this "chore."

Suddenly, there was a commotion on the road in front of us.

Moreda came to an abrupt halt, catching Delai unaware, for she collided with our older sister. I just hid behind her cloak and looked around to see what was happening.

I saw a group of people standing a few feet from a person that I could tell was covered from head to toe. Even his face was unseen. The crowd was jeering; some were pointing to the figure. Others were yelling at him and motioning him to leave the area. The individual seemed to be struggling to stay on his feet. Moreda finally came to her senses and, grabbing our hands, she pulled Delai and me along the path, putting as much distance from the crowd as she could while keeping us away from the man who, for some reason, seemed to be bringing great ire down upon himself.

As we inched closer, I could see the form was a man who, by that time, had fallen to the ground. I could also hear some sounds coming from him. While Moreda pulled us past him, part of the covering fell off of his face, and I noticed that much of his face seemed to be drooping to one side. His mouth was moving, but his words were not coming out clearly. Delai cried out in fear, and Moreda kept pulling us away from the scene. As we headed toward the house, I looked back to see some people in the crowd, which was continuing to grow larger, had begun throwing stones at the heaped form on the ground.

When we reached the house, Delai ran to Mother crying and trying to talk. Mother held her and tried to soothe her while she was trying to listen to Moreda explain what we had witnessed.

When Delai finally calmed down enough and Moreda had finished her account of the ordeal, Mother took Delai and me, sat us on her lap, and began to explain.

"Children, the man in the street has a disease which is known as tzara'at. We are not certain how it is that some people get the disease while others do not. Years ago, our people were warned that when people are afflicted with tzara'at, they were to live away from other people so they would not spread the disease through the camp or town. If anyone afflicted with tzara'at saw that they were getting close to people, they were to say the word 'unclean,' which would warn the people to keep their distance."

At that time, I squeezed Mother's arm to get her attention. As she looked down into my eyes, I spoke, "Mother, he was saying something, but since some of his face seemed to be falling down toward his neck, the words could not come out clearly. He was probably saying 'unclean,' but no one could understand him."

"Gaius, that could possibly be exactly what the man was trying to say. And the fact that his skin was falling off of his face tells me that he has had this disease for a very long time. When some people see a person who is entirely covered in robes and cloth, they should know that the person is very ill, but it doesn't seem like they are willing to listen. They, like most of us, are afraid of things that we don't understand, and fear makes us do many things that we wouldn't normally do in any situation, or at least that is what we tell ourselves. Without being a part of the crowd, not any of us actually know what we would do if we were put in that position."

Now, coming back to the time when I found myself in the possible position of that man afflicted with tzara'at and, in turn, putting members of my family in the role of that crowd, I wondered about the thoughts that would be running through the minds of people when they eventually learn the truth. After all, not any of us knew what we would be facing in the coming weeks.

As the color came back into my mother's face, she grasped my hand and said that I needed to go at once to see the cohen (priest). He would do an examination of the area, and we would be able to find out exactly what it was, whether it was something serious.

Giesell had wanted to accompany me, but Mother explained that I had to go alone. If it did turn out to be tzara'at and she had been with me, the priest could declare her to be unclean as well.

I began the walk to the temple while Giesell waited with Mother. The walk itself, I don't remember; everything just seemed to be a big blur. The thoughts that were running through my mind seemed to be overwhelming me. I felt as if my head were spinning.

I do recall the moment that I stood before the cohen. He called for two others to come forward as witnesses. They stared at the rash on my neck and nodded in agreement, stating aloud that I needed, at once, to separate myself from all people. I would need to return to them in seven days for them to see whether the rash had begun to clear up or had gotten worse. If they were not sure about the rash at that time, there would be another seven days of waiting. Depending on how bad it looked at that time, there was a possibility they could actually say for positive that it was tzara'at or simply a rash.

I began the journey back to Mother and Giesell slowly. Finding myself standing by an empty field, I stopped for a few minutes, sitting on the ground, my mind again racing with thoughts and wonderings of what the outcome would be if this turned out to be tzara'at. How would it affect my life? How long would I have this disease? Would I be able to recover from it, or would I have it for the rest of my life? Was this a deadly disease? How long would I live? I couldn't go back to the Guard, so how was I going to support my family? I couldn't even go back to the house. Where was

I going to live? What would Giesell do? Would she go back to her parent's house, or would my parents be willing to take her into their home? How did I get this disease? What was going on? The questions continued to race in my mind. But for all the questions which came to my mind, I could not find any answers.

At that moment, I felt something growing inside of me; a feeling, well, it was like anger. Even on my worst days, I didn't plan for this to happen. I would never have believed that it was possible. It had been years since we had even heard the word "tzara'at." I thought that it was something that happened long ago and maybe someone had found a cure. Maybe I was naïve, but after one occurrence when I was five, we just never heard of the disease being anywhere near us.

After a few moments of feeling lost and alone, I shook my head and muttered to myself, "Enough!" I got to my feet and continued on my journey, thinking, *Why am I focused on the negative? I should believe that this rash would be gone by the time I return to the cohen in seven days.* Thinking of my mother and the faith of our people, I remembered the words spoken by David, "I always set Adonai before me; with Him at my right hand, I can not be moved." I began a discussion with Adonai asking Him to remain at my side.

As I walked up to the house, Giesell, Mother, and Abba came out of the house. I stopped about ten feet away, and Mother reached out to hold Giesell from coming any closer. She acted as if she wanted to shake off the hand and rush to me, but I shook my head and motioned for her to stop. I explained what I had been told by the cohen and the return visit that would either be good news or bad news. Until we knew for sure, I would have to be on my own. Abba suggested that I go toward the foot of the mountain outside of town. I would be away from people yet close enough that they would be able to check on me from time to time. He could go back to the Guard and get a tent that we could get set up for me. He would also let the general and other superior officers know that I would be away for a while longer. Mother said that she and Giesell would go back to our house and pick up a few things for me to use. They would also bring some food for the evening meal.

I took off for the mountain, gathering wood as I went; I knew that I would need it for the coolness of the night. Abba arrived after I had been sitting on a big boulder for a few minutes. Without getting really close to me, he helped set up the tent so I would have shelter. The rainy season was not going to be starting for a few months, but the shelter would keep me out of the sun. The trees were further up the slope of the mountain. There were bunches of shrubs close by, so I would be out of sight of passersby as I did my personal business.

After the tent was in place, Abba and I sat separately but within a small enough distance that we were able to speak to one another. Not that we had too much to say at that point. He mentioned that in speaking to my superiors, he had told them that I had taken ill and would need to be out for a little while longer than we had first thought. They sent their respects and hoped that I would be well soon.

Giesell and Mother showed up a little while after, bringing dinner with them. Mother decided that we would eat together as a family. While she had brought some utensils and a bowl for me to keep, I noticed that she had brought a few squares of cloth. At first, I could not figure out why but as the evening meal went on, I noticed that, out of habit, I touched a particular spoon or bowl. Mother would take that cloth in her hand and pick up the item, removing it from the area and placing it into a separate bag that she had behind her. I can't remember how many times I had to apologize, but she would always smile her forgiveness, stating that she knew that it would be difficult, at first, for me to remember these things.

After that day, for many months, I always noticed that Mother would always carry extra cloth with her just in case.

They left soon after the meal was completed, wanting to get home before darkness fell. I watched them walk away, and then I was alone with my thoughts.

Not long after the sun went down, I felt the early evening chill set in. Getting up, I pulled out the heavier cloak that Giesell had packed for me, wrapping it around my shoulders. I stirred the fire and added a couple of good-sized sticks to the heap, then sat down, watching the flames. I don't really believe that I was thinking about any one thing. There were a thousand things running through my mind, and I wondered if this was how it was going to be for the entire week. As for how long I sat there just staring at the fire and thinking, I am not really sure. I do remember that I did not sleep much that night.

As I was awakened the next morning by the sound of birds chirping in the nearby bushes, the thought of how my life had changed over the past year came to my mind. After the marriage ceremony took place for Giesell and me, the time we spent with her family or with family members of mine had considerably become less as one day passed on into another. I realize that we were a couple now, beginning our own family, working on making a home together, and were expecting to spend time trying to build our own way in this life. But we still had things to learn from the older generation. They may have had tribulations in their past, and by knowing the steps that were taken to make it through those times, we that have come after them might be able to make it through circumstances that come our way. I began to wish that I had spent more time with Abba, and maybe, I would know how to face the test on which I was about to embark.

By the way Mother, Abba, and Giesell looked when they arrived a while later, I could tell that they didn't get much rest either. Abba was on his way to the Guard, and he only sat for a few minutes. Mother had brought food for us to eat, but I wasn't feeling very hungry.

After about one hour of trying to converse with me, Mother mentioned to Giesell that they should go ahead and get to our house. They had to pack up our belongings. I took that to mean that Giesell had agreed to stay with them for the week. When everything had been cleared up, we could find another place, maybe even one closer to their house. We could then spend more time with each other because people never know what you will have to face. It's best to have someone near that will be able to help in any situation.

Once again, I found myself on my own. It had been quite a long time since I had that much spare time. Before long, I was at my wits' end. What was going to occupy my time for the next six days if I couldn't even find something that I could do on the very first one?

At that point, thoughts of my training kicked in, and I began the drill that I had been leading the trainees through these last few months. I ran up the mountain, okay, not the entire way up the mountain. I did put a bit of distance between my camp and the point where I grew tired and had to take a rest. I looked over the countryside and saw people walking around town, heading to wherever they were going. Others were out feeding the herds and flocks while there were farmers going about their business of tending to their crops.

Presently, I took a walk down the mountain noticing all the different plants and growth around me. These things I knew were part of the country, but I had never just taken the time to pay attention. That got me thinking that I could use these next few days to travel around the countryside. As long as I stayed a considerable distance from other people, I would be alright and wouldn't be putting others' health or well-being at risk.

When I made it back to my tent, I picked up some of the food that Mother had left for me. For the first time since all this tzara'at scare had begun, I had a clear mind and knew what I wanted to do for the next few days. I was still focused on my upcoming trip when Mother and Giesell arrived from town.

They had brought a few more bundles of clothes and things that I would need. They noticed a difference in me, and I began to tell them what I wanted to do to pass the time until I had to present myself to the cohen. They shared the food with me as we discussed the need to keep my distance, cover my body, and stay safe. Mother seemed to accept the idea, knowing that this activity would keep me from playing out scenarios in my mind. Giesell, on the other hand, was worried that what I was speaking about doing with my time was foolishness. For a grown man to aimlessly walk about the countryside was just not heard of; it was not done. What would people think? They would believe him to be some kind of drifter—one who did not have a place to belong.

I tried to calm her by saying that it would be better than me just sitting around a campfire or inside a tent, passing the hours away until I had to go back to the synagogue. I would take all precautions and be aware of my surroundings at all times. I would be back in a few days, and we would be ready to face whatever came our way together as a family. That seemed to quieten her fears, but she mentioned the fact that it would be a great idea if this was actually a trip that we could do together as a family.

Wanting so much to take her in my arms and hug away her fears, I made myself stay where I was. I looked at her with all the sincerity that I could, telling her that I, too, wished that this was something that we could do together. At this point, it could not. But I said that while I had to do this on my own, when my rash was cleared, and we were again able to be together, I would take her on the same journey, maybe one even better. I would point out to her all the wondrous things that I had seen and wanted to share with her. We would walk down the roads that would lead to the towns and cities that we knew were so much more than what we had seen while growing up in Sh'khem. By that time, Giesell was beginning to dream as big as me.

Eventually, Mother spoke of returning to the house to begin preparations for the evening meal and bringing back enough for the next few days so I would have provisions for the trip. Giesell said that she would help with that; I would not have to be hungry while I was away.

When they walked back to town, I began going through the bundles that they had left for me. I set aside a couple of things that I would use before the morning, then began putting things together for the trip.

Hours later, I noticed the three figures coming from town and knew that this was the time that Abba would have something to say about this fantasy of mine. I was totally shocked when he agreed that this would be the best use of my time since I could not do much of anything else. Maybe I would be able to find what it was that was missing from my life, and when I returned, I would be willing to do what needed to be done for my family. (Sometimes, I wondered where he came up with the thoughts behind his speeches. Was there something wrong with just saying that he thought I was doing a good thing? Or was this another "abba" thing—when you have to strengthen your children's resolve to do better? I don't really know, but maybe this was the only way he knew to show that he cared for me.)

We sat and had a family meal together. Giesell has set her bundle down a bit to the side, stating that it was the food for the trip, and she wanted me to stay safe while I was out there on my own. Both she and my mother looked like they wanted to come closer to give me hugs and kisses but knew that they shouldn't. They stayed a little longer than they had the night before yet still left before the sun went below the horizon.

Before he left, Abba motioned to a bag that he had placed on the dirt beside the tent and stated that he thought I could use it while I was "out in the world." After a few more words of wisdom, more "please stay safe" messages, they left for town. Giesell turned around a couple of times while they were still in sight to wave at me. I waved back while wishing with all my heart that I could go running to them and hug all three of them as tightly as I could.

As I turned away from watching their departure, my gaze fell on the bundle that Abba had placed on the ground. I picked it up and opened it. Once I saw what was placed in the bundle, I understood exactly what my father had been trying to say. In my hands, I held the drawings that I had made when I was younger, along with more paper and charcoal with which to draw other buildings. I felt the tears welling up in my eyes. I began to think that Abba actually thought that I could accomplish big things. Maybe this was his way of telling me that I should have followed this dream of mine instead of going into the military to please him. Or maybe this *was* his way of letting me know how much he cared for me!

The next morning at sunrise, I was on my way.

Four days later, I was back at my tent, unpacking my things to settle in for the next day—the last day that I would be isolated from my family. I had not noticed any difference in the rash; it didn't seem to be spreading, and I was not feeling any other symptoms that might tell me that it was getting worse. After the days that I had traveled around, I was so excited about the possibilities of taking Giesell around where I had been and even further north. I had only made it to Shomron since I only had a short time. But to think about what I had seen and witnessed, knowing that there were bigger towns and even greater cities to visit, I felt the urgent desire to begin a new chapter in our life together. We were going to be able to see every part of our country and even beyond those borders. We were going to live the life that I knew we deserved, and I was going to find a way to make that happen for both of us.

As it had been for the last four nights, I found it hard to sleep. There were so many thoughts and dreams going around in my head. Realizing that there could be so much more for Giesell and me, I know that we would be giving up the life that we had made for ourselves here, and it would be hard to leave the family that was so close to us.

Of course, we would come back to visit and share our experiences with them. It wasn't as if we wanted to disappear from their lives altogether. I still wanted to know if Abba and Mother were healthy, and somewhere deep, I wanted them to know that I would always be there when they needed me. But I also wanted to travel with Giesell. I wanted us to go places that we wanted to go and to be able to see what we wanted to see.

I was confident that this was what I was meant to do. Now that I was old enough, Abba would not be able to run my life. I needed to take control and do what I wanted to do. It would be rough for a while; I was not sure what I would do in order to support us during the time of transition, as all I was trained for was the military. I remained unshaken by the knowledge that I could be a success.

The sun crept slowly over the horizon, and I began stirring around, getting myself together to face this day and the trip to see the cohen. After my morning run, I refreshed myself and gathered my things. I placed them in the tent. I would be able to stop by and pack up the remainder of my things, along with the tent, and head for home to see everyone. I had a few pieces of bread left over, which I ate, drinking some water from the stream.

Within two hours, I was heading to the courtyard of the synagogue. Soon after that, I was back, sitting in front of the tent staring at the ashes of the fire that I had put out not so long ago before I began my trip. Conflict seemed to be raging inside my head. I had no idea what I was going to do. How was I going to break the news to Giesell and my parents? What reactions would they have upon hearing the news that I had received?

I sat for hours trying to find the right words to say but to no avail. At about the eleventh hour, I found myself arriving at my parent's house.

I don't know which was worse, the notification that I had tzara'at or the sounds of anguish that came from my wife as I told her and my parents the news of the spreading disease. The fact that it was so severe that the cohen would not even need the extra seven days to inform me that I was indeed afflicted with tzara'at. I had not been able to realize that it had spread because it was on my back, an area that I couldn't see. He explained that I could have possibly been affected with this disease for years before it even manifested itself into a rash, so there was really no way to know exactly how or when I had come in contact with someone or something that was affected. The disbelief in the eyes of Abba spoke volumes, along with the bewilderment that showed on the face of my mother. For those moments following my telling them the matter, the situation continued to spiral out of control. I could hear the agitation building in Giesell's voice as she spoke to me.

"How could this have happened? What are we going to do?

What about the plans that we had to go traveling together? You should have taken me with you this time because it doesn't look like there is going to be a next time. You let me get my hopes up and begin dreaming of an entirely different life that we could have together. And now, I have nothing. I have no husband. I have no life."

Mother moved toward her to attempt to quieten her with words of faith and belief that all things would be made right. Instead of listening, Giesell pushed Mother's hands away, backing off from her before unleashing a tirade against her.

"Don't you try to tell me that this was the plan that Adonai had for your son! I won't believe for a moment that anyone would have purposefully wished this on any person. Why would you believe in a deity who would do such a thing as this? Isn't this 'Adonai' of yours supposed to be merciful and loving? What has Gaius done to deserve this? Even if he had done something wrong, isn't Adonai also forgiving? You can see, can't you—this doesn't just affect him."

I stood there in astonishment, looking at a woman whom I did not recognize. This was not Giesell, the love of my life. I had never before heard her use such a tone with anyone, especially an elder. We had not been raised like that; we were taught that elders were to be revered. All the knowledge that they had learned through their life was something that we could take and use in order to keep from making mistakes in our own life. We were told to show them the respect that they deserved. I would not have believed that it was possible for her to speak in this manner.

Giesell took a quick breath, looking at my mother, and began again, "If you hadn't stopped me from going with Gaius to the cohen, I might have been declared afflicted also; that is what you said. You should have let me go with him, he is my husband, and at least we could have gone through this together. Since you stopped me, look at us now! What have I done to deserve this happening to my husband? What about the plans that we had for a life together? We were going to start a family, but now that is out of the picture. . What will become of me when others find out that I am married to someone who is now affected by tzara'at? Do you think that I am going to be accepted in this town ever again?

"Maybe it wasn't anything that either one of us did. It could have been you. Is Adonai disappointed in the way that you have lived your life? Is your faith in Adonai not strong enough that it would not keep Him from striking down your own son with this horrid disease? Is there something in your past that might be the reason behind all of this? I do recall one of your cohen reading about the punishment of the children for the sins of the parents. What is it that *you* have done?"

At that point, I could tell that both of my parents, especially Abba, were at the end of their patience with Giesell.

"*Enough!*" I spoke with a deliberate resolve in my voice, and I noticed the look of shock on her face as Giesell turned to face me. I remembered the time in my childhood when Mother had explained about the crowd we had witnessed, being so terrified of the one who was afflicted with this horrible disease. I now knew what that one person was feeling when coming face to face with people filled with fear, for that is what I saw when I looked at Giesell. I continued to talk to my wife.

"There is nothing that anyone could have done in order to foresee this happening to me or anyone else. You are fearful; we all are because we have come face to face with something that we don't understand. We don't perceive any meaning as to why this has happened. We don't see what the outcome might be for us. It's like trying to find our way through a strange house where there is no light; we cannot see anything; we don't know what is in front of us.

"The cohen said that there seems to be no reason why one person gets the disease while others in the same family or in the same community do not. It is not to be considered a punishment for any one person or any one thing, so trying to put the blame on any of us is not the right thing to do at this time.

"This is something that will have to be dealt with in accordance with the laws of our people. The law states that I need to be away from all people so as not to affect them. That we know is something that I am going to have to do.

"You cannot put the blame on Mother for stopping you from coming with me. I would never have agreed to let you come with me. Even if you had, the cohen would have seen that you did not have the rash and would have told you to stay your distance from me until they could have found out the results. But I would never have allowed you to accompany me."

I reached out my hand toward her and spoke tenderly. "This disease, we don't know anything about it, but I remember from my childhood seeing a man that had been afflicted. I do not know how long he had to deal with the pain and the agony that I saw on his face. I don't want to go through anything as he had to do, and there is certainly no way that I was going to put you through that life.

"We can go about this in a reasonable fashion and keep it a family matter. You can stay here, and I will leave this area. The cohen spoke of a camp on the other side of Mt. Ebal. It is far enough away from here that no one will know of my condition. Since everyone around is aware of the dream that I have had since I was young, in the designing of buildings, you say that I have decided to go throughout the countryside. They might believe that is the reason that I left town. Abba and Mother, I am sure, will have you stay with them as you are part of this family if that is what you want to do. What you say to your family is up to you. It is in our power as to how we handle what has been thrust upon us."

I looked at Abba and addressed him, "I will give you the few sheep and goats that we have to help with any additional expenses that will occur with this added responsibility. If you find someone who wants the house, please take care of that."

Mother came a little bit closer but still stayed a distance away. "I am proud of you, bar. I know that this time will be difficult, but your faith will make you strong and allow you to come through this, no matter how long it will take you. I will gather some things for you to take on your journey, and we can sit out here for our last meal together before you leave."

I thanked her as she went back into the house. Abba stood there for a few minutes, looking at me while holding on to the railing in front of the house. He seemed to have aged as we had been standing there. By the looks of things, he was having a hard time keeping himself upright, his knees seemed to be shaky, and his whole body was trembling. What thoughts were going through his mind, I do not know, nor did he speak them aloud to me. Yet, thinking back on what Giesell had spoken about, it may be the fault of the parents that the son was being punished; I could not help but think that was what was weighing on his mind.

Those times earlier in my life when he was so critical about what we were being taught by my mother, the nights of Shabbat when he sat outside the house instead of spending time with his family. Was he thinking that if he had done things differently that we would not be facing this problem? Did he believe that if he had stronger faith in Adonai, that tzara'at would never have been allowed to invade his family? Maybe that was exactly what he was thinking; I will never know since whatever he imagined in his mind as he stood there looking at me, he did not put into words. He looked at me with a sadness that I had never before seen on his face. Then silently, he turned and made his way slowly through the doorway.

I turned back to Giesell and noticed that she was quietly studying me. She then spoke, "I will do as you say. I will not mention this to anyone. After a while, they will forget that we were even together for this short period, and I can move on to the life that I want.

"As for you, your family, and your faith in Adonai, that is for you but not for me. I cannot believe in such a deity that would give me a husband and then take him away from me, especially in such a way as this.

"You can still give the goats and sheep to your father, and he can do what he wills with the house that we once shared. I will go home to my parents' house, where I will stay." As she went into the house, she spoke again, "Goodbye, Gaius. I will tell your mother that you will not be staying for dinner."

With that, she was gone, along with any thought that I might have about the family life that we were to build. I started wondering what had happened to the love that we had felt for each other, or was that just an illusion that I had in my mind? I know that it wasn't on my part, but the way that Giesell had just given up on me, given up on us, the doubts about the love that she should have had for me began to creep into my head. All those thoughts that I had months before about us being made for each other, how even with our faults, I knew that our love would be able to work, to hold us together no matter what we would face in our life together. I don't know how I could have been so wrong.

I turned and slowly walked back to my tent. There would be no family meal that night.

Dawn was beginning to break as I finished folding the tent and bundling it together with my few belongings when I looked up to see Mother walking up the path. She stopped a few feet away and dropped a small bundle to the ground.

"Your abba is going to sell a couple of the sheep to the Guard to cover the cost of the tent and will be giving the remainder of it to Giesell. I am sorry, Gaius; she collected her things last night and left for her parents' house."

Grimacing slightly, I spoke, "Yes, I got the impression that was what she had planned after saying what she did to me, to us, last night. I wonder what the future will hold for her."

"Yes, bar, I wonder what the future holds for all of us."

Seeing the look of love and longing to be close to me in my mother's eyes brought a lump to my throat, and I felt the sting of tears.

She raised her hand toward me and spoke the last words that I would hear from her lips for a while. "Even this is in control of Adonai. He will give you the strength to persevere, and He will supply what you need. I will visit you as often as I can. I know in my heart that you will be coming back home to me, and I will be able to hold you in my arms again. Until then, know that I love you, and so does Abba."

"I love you, Mother. Please give my love to Abba. If you would, please keep in touch with Giesell. I would like to hear how she is doing if that is possible. Tell all my sisters that I wish them well in their lives, that I love them and would have loved to have seen them before I had to go away."

With our goodbyes said, I gathered all the bundles, tying them and swinging them over my shoulders. Mother and I walked down the lane, as close to each other as we could, just glad that we had these last few moments together. As we reached the turn in the lane, I reached out to her as she did to me—not touching, but each of us knowing that feeling of family intimacy. "I love you, Mother!"

"I love you, Gaius! I will see you soon." With that, she turned to the left, and I turned to the right. As the distance grew between us, I felt the tears running down my face. At that particular moment, for the first time in my life, I felt such an intense emotion of loneliness I couldn't find the proper words to explain it.

CHAPTER TWO

I reached the camp four days later. It wasn't that it was so far to travel; in fact, I could have made the trip in less than an hour. I was not in any hurry to begin this part of my life's journey—I was not ready to leave the life that I had been living. After leaving Mother at the crossroads when she was going back to town, I decided to stick around where I had been staying for a few days more.

I did my morning runs and did some walking every day, ate from the provisions that I had, and slept on the ground. I spent a lot of time in thought and self-pity. Soon, I was tired of that, and on the fourth day, I picked up my things and went for that short walk to the camp, where I was immediately welcomed by those who had been there for a while.

In the hours and days to come, I would learn of their stories, their lives before all the upheaval of being afflicted with tzara'at had ended the times that they had known.

There was a couple who had been living in the same community when they had become afflicted, David and Tirtzah (Tirzah). They were from the north country, but past generations had lived in the countryside around Bethlehem.

David was named after King David of Yerushalayim, and Tirtzah was named after the town where her family had lived for generations. They had been married for about five years when the tzara'at had made its presence known, and they had moved to this camp three years ago.

There was Zeresh and Rivkah (Rebecca), another couple who had met in a camp on the other side of the Yarden (Jordan), near the Gerasene district, and had made their way here to be closer to her family in Sh'khem. They were able to walk into town and visit with the family two or three times a month. They had conducted their own marriage ceremony a few months before settling into camp.

As soon as I met Zeresh, I thought that I might have met him, or at least seen him, some years ago, but I could not remember where it was that it might have been. I thought that I would recall the meeting sometime soon.

The last occupant of the camp was Yo'ed (Joed), whom I was told was a loner and kept away from everyone. When introduced to him, I was reminded of Ammi, the boy from my childhood. He had the same dark skin that Ammi had, and I thought that they might have been from the same region of the country, south of Isra'el.

I was trying to remember the name of the country of which Ammi had spoken years ago, stating that his family in which generations long ago had lived. But it was too far in my past for me to recall what he had told me.

Since Yo'ed was unwilling to speak to the others, much less tell of where he had lived before coming to the camp, the two couples liked to spend time making up stories of the life that Yo'ed had previously. They had come up with some really interesting background beliefs about this silent member of their community. There was one in which David talked about Yo'ed being the prince of a country to the south, whose father had some of his people transport him out to this place so the rest of the people would not find out about the disease.

Other stories were that he was not infected at all. He was working for the Roman government, or maybe he was working against the Roman government. He was a spy for the Zealots—the opposition movement that wanted to bring a revolt against the Roman ruling party. He lived quite a way away from the others in the camp and had been known to be wandering around at night. That was when he would meet his friends, and they would make plans to attack Rome.

I thought that story was ridiculous! Why would anyone want to be placed in a colony of people who were infected with the disease that we had, I am not sure. It wasn't like we were going to rally the townspeople behind us and take over the city of Rome or any other town for that matter. But I guess with not too much to do during the day, there was plenty of time for imaginations to start speculating on all sorts of things.

I know that they imagined most of these things about Yo'ed, trying to put a reasoning to the fact that he did not confide in them as they had shared their past lives with each other. I believe that is just the way that he was; whether he was raised that way or something had happened in his life to make him become like that, I am not sure. He wanted to keep to himself, not allowing any intimacy to grow between him and anyone else. Maybe he thought it would be better for all concerned if no feelings were ever shared. I imagine that there are some people like that, but I would not have any idea if I could ever be one of them.

A few times, I had tried to talk to Yo'ed, speaking of a boy that I had known from my childhood being as he was and thinking that they might have been from the same country. But all he would do is sit and stare at the horizon. After that, it was as if there were only five of us that lived at that camp; Yo'ed acted like he did not exist in our world, so we left him to his. Some days, though, I felt sorry that he wanted things to go that way, being on his own. Many things that we have to endure in our lives are just easier if we have someone with whom to share them.

There seemed to be quite a lot of talk going on from people who were traveling the roads. David and Zeresh always came back from town with talk that they had heard as they made their way to and from the well. There seemed to be some people willing to discuss the thought of the Romans being removed from our country; we as a people should be able to rule ourselves.

As I settled into life there, the couples would bring me into their conversations on all the workings of the camp. Every other afternoon, the couples took turns making a trip into town to the well to get a supply of water. There was a small cart on which the water vessels were placed, and the guys would pull the cart. I guess they went as teams for the companionship more than anything else because that trip could take a great deal of time when you had the weight of even half full water vessels on that cart.

Every day after breaking my fast, I would go for either a run or a walk, most times up the mountain. I realized that it might not be long at all until I lost the strength and ability to do these activities. I wanted to see the countryside while I had the chance. On a few occasions, I would walk out toward the east. I had heard if I walked far enough, I would come to the Yarden River. I always thought that it would be a grand sight to see.

When we were growing up, Mother would tell us the very ancient stories of how our people had come to this land that we now call our home. For many years, many more years than our people had been in Paras, we had been in the country called Egypt. A great leader by the name of Moshes (Moses), following the direction of Adonai, delivered the people out of that country. After forty years of traveling and camping in the desert, Adonai directed the next leader, Y'hoshua (Joshua), to lead the people the remainder of the way into the land that He had promised to the descendants of Avraham. Y'hoshua, along with the Cohanim and the help of Adonai, led the people over the Yarden River.

I thought that if I traveled to the river and then followed it down to the south, I might actually see the stones that had been left as a witness of how Adonai had led His people through the river into their homeland. Now that I have the time to do that, it would be a wonderful thing to accomplish. And what a story to be able to pass down to my children and their children. Soon after that thought had entered my mind, I recalled that at this point in my life, there would be no children with whom I could share that story. That was just a dream from my past, which now no longer existed.

Mother would come out for a day of visiting every week. She would bring provisions for me. After meeting the others of the camp, she began to bring provisions that would help supply their need for nourishment. Then, she would sit and talk to me, bringing me news of Abba and how he was getting along with his work and the men. He was able to sell the house to a family that had just moved into town from the west. When she heard from my sisters, she would always let me know that they had asked how I was doing. They were all imploring Adonai for my healing so that I could return to the family. When I asked about Giesell, Mother would say that she was doing fine.

After about two weeks of getting the same answer to my question about Giesell, I decided that I would walk back to Sh'khem to see for myself. One morning, I gathered the clothing that would be needed to cover myself from head to foot, leaving only a small opening for me to see. Knowing that walking around the mountain would take longer, I decided to walk over part of the mountain. In the days past, while I was out on my run, I began to find little ways that would lead to Sh'khem. I found that I was able to get to town in a shorter time. As I came close to the edge of the woods, I took the clothing that I had brought and put it on to cover myself.

When I got closer to town, there were people out and about, so I kept as far behind them as I could. When the crowd began to get larger, I got off the road, pretending I needed to rest. In a few minutes, they would have passed, continuing on their way, which gave me some space for walking. I knew that all I had to do was say the word "unclean," and they would have parted in order for me to pass by. I was not at the point where I wanted to draw attention to myself. Maybe one day I would be willing to do so, but that wasn't this day. With all the stopping, it took me longer to reach the center of town than I had expected. It was around the sixth hour (noon) when I found myself just down the lane from Giesell's family home. I sat down behind some bushes, out of sight, but still able to see the coming and going of people from the house.

Before the ninth hour had arrived, I noticed Giesell walking around from the side of the house. She headed down the lane and met up with a man whose back was turned toward me, so I was unable to see if I recognized him. They continued toward town, talking as if they were old friends. As I knew that I didn't want to wait there until they returned, since I didn't know how long that would be, I rose to my feet and followed them from a distance. They continued on for a short time, then turned toward a house that seemed to be having a gathering. There was a crowd of people on the outside, and it definitely sounded like there was even a larger group on the inside. Instead of going any closer, I turned to begin my trip to the camp.

While walking back, I began to wonder what kind of gathering would be happening in the middle of the afternoon. I guess it could have been a late midday meal, maybe a family celebration, or there could have been a death in the family. The more I thought about it, I realized that it probably wasn't a death because the sounds from the crowd were not those of people in mourning. That was more of a celebration.

At that moment, I did not know how right I was.

Five days later, Mother made an unscheduled visit. She looked more tired than she usually did after her walk from town. While she was talking, I could tell that the strain of her coming out to see me was coming at the high price of her health. We discussed the possibility that she would stay at the house, and I would make the journey into town to visit with her and Abba. As I finished speaking on the matter, I saw that there were tears in her eyes. I asked what was wrong.

She broke down, sobbing uncontrollably, and I wanted so much to rush to her side, to hold her and comfort her. After a few minutes, she was able to speak.

"Since Giesell had moved back to her parent's house, there had been rumors going around town about the exact reason that her marriage was broken and she had returned home. Many were saying that you were a coward and could not face a life in the town, that you had failed in your military career, and that is why you decided to go wandering all over the country drawing lines on paper, expecting to be some great builder. Abba and I had our suspicions about how these rumors had started, but we have kept that to ourselves. It would have served no purpose for us to make known who it was that began saying these things. Others thought if you were actually doing something like that, you could have at least taken your wife with you.

"Your abba had been hearing all the talk behind his back every day. He couldn't take the thought of the entire community thinking that his son had run from his responsibilities as a husband and as a military leader. All of that had really begun to take a toll on him.

"Then, we heard the news that Giesell had married another

man a few days ago. There was some great celebration as the man that she married was a leader of the council and was well-known in the community. That was one more thing that Abba couldn't take—the knowledge that she would actually move on so quickly after the breaking with you.

"While he was out on the field training some new men on how to use swords and spears on the battlefield, he stepped in between two fighters and was killed. The two trainees said that things happened so fast that they could not stop what they were doing at the time." She began to cry again. "I don't know if he was thinking about what was going on in front of him or if he was still worried about this family business. Maybe that was what kept him from realizing how close he had really gotten to the action."

I was shocked and did not know what to say, how to react. Why had Abba put himself in the position of being that close to men with swords? He had been in the service for so many years he would have known not to step in between two fighters until they had dropped their weapons down to their sides.

Then, my thoughts went back to the words that Mother had spoken about the talk of the town getting into Abba's mind, and my brain became overwhelmed with ideas. My mind went back to the last night with Giesell and the words that she had spoken that it might have been possible that Adonai had been disappointed in the way that Abba had lived his life. Were those the thoughts that had been with him for this whole time? Had he been blaming himself for what had happened to me? I know that he had not been out to see me since I had arrived at the camp. I had just thought that he had been too busy. With me being out, more responsibility would have fallen upon him and other officers. Those obligations alone would be crushing to the most gallant of men. And then, there were responsibilities that he had as a husband, trying to keep up with those things that Mother could not do by herself.

I continued to remember that last night at the house and the thoughts that I, myself, had when looking at Abba. Had he regretted those times when he put work before family? Did he begin thinking that this situation that we were facing was because of something that he had done? I wish that I had taken the time to sit down with him and have a long conversation, one that was long overdue. A talk that was now impossible.

Could this sickening incident have been avoided if there hadn't been all that talk about Giesell and me? It got to be too much for Abba, and that was the only way that he knew to rid himself of all the troubles. After all, he was a military man and a very proud one at that. With all the years that he had put into the service, I could see where he would have difficulty knowing that not only were his superiors judging him for what his son had done but also that subordinates were whispering behind his back.

What was with all the rumors? Didn't people have better things to do than to wonder why I was no longer in town or why Giesell had moved back in with her parents? How could we have gotten to the point where she would even consider marriage to another man? It had been only a month since I left town.

Now, with Abba gone, what would Mother do? Where would she go? As the only son, I felt that I had a responsibility to care for my mother. But in the situation that I was in, there was no way that I would be able to care for her. I felt that I had failed the entire family.

As she got up to leave, I spoke, asking if she would give me a few minutes. She sat back down. I asked her what the Guard had done when all this had happened. She mentioned that two of the officers had come by the house to inform her of the accident. She, in turn, asked if they could dispatch a courier to take the news to K'far-Nachum to let her daughter and her husband know as they were ones of the family that lived closer than any of the others. They agreed to send word, so Mother expected Moreda to arrive in a week. The burial had been as it would have been for any military man; a lot of officers, and ones that he had trained, had been in attendance. The entire company had sent their condolences, and the neighbors had come to the house to sit with her for a few days of mourning. I felt so bad that I could not have been there at this time of hurting.

While Mother sat and rested from her journey, I went over to David and Tirtzah's tent and spoke to them briefly about what had happened, along with the plan that I had to go back to town until things could be decided about my mother. I would leave the tent and my possessions there in camp, in their care, and would return as soon as I could. They agreed to watch over things and offered their sympathy for my family and me.

I returned to Mother and told her what I had planned. I did not want to have her believe that she was on her own. I might not be able to hold and comfort her as a bar should be able to do, but I would be able to keep her safe while she was in her own home. I asked her to stay and rest for a while; then, we would head back across the mountain if she thought that she had enough strength to make it some way up instead of around the foot of the mountain. I explained that it would be less walking in the long run, but she would also need the toughness of a military man. She said that she would be willing to try, and as she rested, I began to look around for a sturdy enough stick that could be used as a staff. It would help Mother over the paths that we would take and keep her steady on her feet since I would be unable to get close to her. I gathered my usual coverings and a few clothing changes, and about an hour later, we began our trek up the mountain. We did not have to go far until I mentioned to Mother that we were at the point where we could turn to the left and stay on the path that would lead us to the spot where we could walk down to the road that would take us into town.

By the time dusk was falling, we had turned down the lane toward the house. Mother went inside to light the fire as I stood right outside the door. I noticed the wood was stacked at the side of the room. Mother explained that a few neighbors had sent their sons over to make sure that she had enough wood and that there was more piled up on the side of the house. The lanterns had been filled with oil, and the room was lit as I remembered from the last time that I had been there. As Mother began her rituals for bed, I went around the side of the house, just away from the front entrance, and made my bed for the night. In the morning, I would be able to set up a makeshift tent that would keep me as comfortable as possible.

After dawn arrived, I began to unpack a large cloth that I would use as a shelter, working on getting it set up against the front of the house. I turned the opening toward the path that led up from the lane to the doorway so I would be able to see who was approaching the house. I had always been a light sleeper and knew that if anyone came up the path late in the day or throughout the night, I would be able to hear them. This is the only way I knew for sure that I would be able to protect my mother.

Five days had passed since we had made the trip from camp, and I was now settled into the routines of the day outside the house. I would get up early and dress for my training. I would walk over toward the foot of the mountain where I had camped the week between the visits to the cohen. There, I would follow the path up the side of the mountain as I had before, sitting for a while looking at the countryside as it began to awaken from its slumber. I would then head back down and settle in my shelter before the crowds began their business of the day.

Mother was making it through the days the best that was possible, considering all the condolence calls that were continuing to pour in even then. But each day, I noticed that the visits were tapering off and realized that soon, there would be no one to come and spend time with my mother.

Another thing that had become a habit for me is that I would take out the piece of mirror that I carried around and look to see if there was any clearing of the rash. I was unable to find any relief and then noticed a new spreading of the rash on my left arm. That day Mother noticed it and immediately turned back into the house. A few minutes later, she came out and headed down the path. I inquired as to where she was going at that time of the morning, and she said that she was going to speak to the cohen on my behalf. As she walked away, I began to wonder what she thought the cohen would be able to do for me. They did not have any special oils that they could put on a person who was afflicted with tzara'at. If they did have such an oil, I would have requested that on my first visit, which would mean on the second visit, I would have clear skin. That, in turn, would have me, along with Giesell, still living in our own home, and Abba would be continuing his life with Mother.

For a woman of my mother's age, I noticed that once her mind is set on doing something, there is no stopping her. She was gone no longer than an hour when I saw her coming back down the lane to the house. I could tell that the meeting that she had with the cohen went very well.

As she entered the yard, she spoke to me of the words that she had spoken, the prayers that she had asked the cohen and his brethren to say on my behalf. Adonai needed to heal her son; she did not believe that this was His will that I should be suffering. There had to be a miracle. They agreed to send special prayers for the healing of Gaius, the one afflicted with tzara'at. They would entreat Adonai to rid the body of all the rash and make me clean again.

As she finished the details of the visit, I observed someone coming down the path. She noticed that I was looking past her and turned to see what had caught my attention. What I thought was one person turned out to be a couple, and the smaller of the two, I recognized the gait as she walked toward us. Moreda!

At that same moment, Mother recognized her also and started walking toward the figures. Moreda began running. They met up and embraced each other tightly. I only wish that I could have joined them. They stood where they were until her husband joined the two, and then, together, they continued to walk toward the house. I grabbed my cloth and began to cover myself completely. By the time they were within speaking distance, I had noticed the uncertainty in Moreda's eyes. I watched as Mother placed her hand on Moreda's arm in what seemed to be a comforting gesture, for suddenly, the uncertainty was gone from her eyes. She smiled at me and began by introducing me to her husband, Shim'on (Simon).

I looked past my sister to see the burly figure of a man whose size was overwhelming to me. But the smile and the friendliness which showed in his eyes put me at ease, and I spoke my hellos to him.

That evening was spent on the outside of the house by all. I know that it was to include me in all that we needed to discuss, and I was grateful for that.

Moreda spoke of the decision that she and Shim'on had made that our mother should come to live with them in K'far-Nachum. They had enough room in the house for her, and they would be able to care for her. Moreda said that she knew that if it were possible for me to care for Mother, I would be the one to do so. But as things were at that point, moving Mother to K'far-Nachum would be the best thing to do. I was always welcome to visit and maybe even move into the area if I felt the need to be closer to family.

There was no need for me to stay here. Being elsewhere would give me a fresh start, and now that Giesell had moved on with her life, it was time for me to do the same.

The next morning, I found myself traveling back to the camp to pick up the things that I had left behind. I spoke to David, Tirtzah, Zeresh, and Rivkah about the decision that had been made in regard to my mother and myself. I decided that the change of scenery was exactly what I needed. K'far-Nachum was a bit farther north than I had ever planned on going, but if it kept me within walking distance of my mother and other members of my family, I would be willing to go there. I was sure that there would be a camp close enough to town. If not, well, I had been on my own before and saw nothing wrong with being alone again.

The four said that if they ever thought of moving, they would think of connecting with me again. At the very least, they would visit every once in a while. I told them that I, too, would make trips back to see them. It wasn't like we were going to lose touch with each other. The number of the tzara'at affliction community was not so overwhelming that we could not find each other in time. Before leaving the area, I made three more trips over to the camp to visit with the friends that I had made.

It took us two months to wrap up all of Mother's affairs and get the house sold. There was a couple that bought it in order to give it to their son and his new wife as a wedding gift. They also took the two old goats and three sheep that still belonged to the family. Shim'on decided to take the lamb and add it to his flock but had stated that they already had enough goats.

Settling in at K'far-Nachum was a little harder than I thought it would be. The countryside was entirely different from where we had lived between the two mountains. There was a small parcel of land next to the house of Shim'on that belonged to his parents.

Shim'on said that I could set up my tent there as no one was using the land. I spoke my thanks to him, glad that I would be able to see Mother whenever I wanted.

I did enjoy walking the shores of the Galil (Galilee). I spent a lot of mornings in the quietness that surrounded me. Out in the distance, I saw the boats as the fishermen went searching for the big catch. Shim'on had two boats out there with his crew of three other men. Most nights, they would spend hours waiting for the nets to be filled so they could bring the fish to the shore by the morning time. Other times, they would be out in the evening to catch enough fish for travelers that might be coming through, needing to camp and eat for the night. By the time they were back at shore, I would be off to my place for some rest while the day was still cool enough to sleep.

Afterward, I would walk up to the house where Moreda and Mother were doing chores. Sewing and cooking seemed to be what consumed Mother's time. Moreda and Shim'on had announced that a baby was on the way, and Mother was thrilled at the thought of a newborn in the house. I believe that was a way that she would be able to put the worries of the past behind her. And while knowing that this was an exciting time for Moreda, I felt a sorrow deep within, knowing that I would never have the same. I didn't want to stand in the way of happiness for my family; therefore, I spoke of going on with my training rituals and took my leave. They were so used to my coming and going that nothing was really said. Just the usual "Please, be careful" and "Enjoy your run" along with Mother's "Gaius, I love you."

I went back to my tent and packed my things. I wanted to get out on my own for a while. That way, the focus at the house would be on the baby coming and all the preparations that went along with that.

I spent the day in the tent, and when evening came, the tent was down, and I was ready for my adventure. I rested overnight and rose before the sun came up. I had written a note stating that I was going traveling for some time, that they didn't need to worry, and that I would take all precautions to stay away from people. I walked over to Moreda's house and spread it out on the ground beside the chair which was outside the front door. I placed a rock on the corner of the paper so any breeze that came along would not blow it away. I knew that Mother still had the habit of carrying the squares of cloth in order to pick up anything that I might have touched. When she would awaken every morning, her habit was to walk out the front door and look to see if I was moving around or if I was still asleep. She would notice the paper and would be able to remove the rock, pick up the paper to read the note and then place the paper in the fire. I knew that she would understand why I needed to go.

After walking up the lane, I set out for Beit-Tzaidah (Bethsaida). The town was just around the edge of the Galil and would be a good place to begin the day.

Over the next few months, I spent time there and then traveled over to Korazin (Chorazin). I then came back through K'far-Nachum and visited with Mother for a few days before heading out to Ginosar (Gennesaret) and Magdala on my way back to Sh'khem. It had been a while since I had left the camp where David, Tirtzah, and the rest of the group resided, and I *had* said that I would keep in touch.

By the time I had arrived, the weather was turning cooler, and I gathered some wood for the fire on my way toward the encampment. It was a bit quieter than I remember, and I noticed that no one came out of the tents when I approached. I thought that maybe I had arrived too early; sometimes, people were known to sleep later than usual. I stopped at a distance from the tent and called out for David. A moment later, I heard movement in the tent to my left and saw the tent flap open.

The figure that emerged was indeed David, but he seemed to be a lot smaller than the person that I had left just a few months ago. He was struggling to walk, and I saw that he was now having to rely on a crutch that had been made out of a tree branch. His left leg was held off the ground; the branch was helping pull his weight along to a chair that sat beside a tree outside the tent. As he lowered himself down, I observed that his facial skin was beginning to slide off the bones, but the smile he tried to give was very recognizable. I came closer to sit on a rock that was beside the chair, greeting my old friend while still trying to hide the shock that I was feeling. Had I been gone that long?

We sat for hours, and David spoke of all that had happened in the time that I had been gone. Considering the loss of muscle from his face, I was surprised that when he spoke, his words were still comprehensible. I set all of that aside and concentrated on the news that he was telling me.

First, Rivkah had gotten worse, and it wasn't long until Tirtzah and Yo'ed did also. They were all dead now, and Zeresh was still breathing, but for how long was anyone's guess. It had been weeks since he was able to sit up, much less get out of his bed. There were a few good people still left in Sh'khem that would fix a bit of extra food and bring it out to the camp; not coming too close, mind you, but to still be able to walk a short distance and find your next meal, along with the water vessel being filled to the brim was a brakhah (blessing).

There was a group of men who were carpenters that had been kind enough to make some beds, small tables, and a few chairs; women who had sewn blankets for them and others that had brought in extra clothing that could be used as they were needed.

Those who had children would often bring them, pulling the carts that had water vessels on them in order to provide water for the camp. There were three different groups that would bring water in the early evening every other day. The supply never ran low, nor did the food that was supplied to those afflicted. David would feed Zeresh as much as he could swallow, and there would still be enough for him to be satisfied.

Many people would stay for a while and talk to him, telling him of the things that were happening around the town and the countryside. There was much news that he was sure I would be interested in hearing.

The marriage of Giesell had not lasted too long, but the reason why was just speculation on the part of which person was telling you the story. A month ago, she had wed again, yet already the rumors were flying around that this one wouldn't last long either. There seemed to be some bad blood between family members that was causing some problems between the couple.

After completing the news of the area, he asked how my family was doing. I spoke of Mother and how she was settling into her life there. Moreda was getting ready to welcome a baby into the family, and Shim'on seemed to be able to support the family and many others with the fishing business that he had in the area. I told him of the seaside and the travels that I had been able to complete.

A little while later, I noticed a figure coming over the incline of the mountain toward the camp. I guess that David and the group had shared with the townspeople the shorter way to get from their places to the campsite. A little further and the person stopped and began to empty the content of her pot into the one that was sitting on a flat rock. David mentioned that this was Dorlas, the wife of a friend of Rivkah's family. She was the one who usually brought the food for the group, even though the cooking responsibilities were shared by a few women in her neighborhood. She had been sick recently, and a couple of other women had stepped in to help with the food distribution at that time. Dorlas had begun the walk again now that she was feeling better.

I told David to sit and that I would go over to retrieve the meal. He warned me not to move too quickly to pick up the pot which sat on the rock; for if I did, it might be a while that I would be standing there holding that pot because Dorlas loved to talk. I grinned as I rose, mentioning to him that I was used to that, as Moreda was the same way. Before walking away, I noticed that David had leaned his head back against the tree and closed his eyes. If he was this bad and still able to care for Zeresh, who was unable to even feed himself, I began wondering how long David had in this life.

As I approached Dorlas, she was pouring the last of what looked to be soup into the pot that had been left on the flat rock on the path. I introduced myself as Phin, part of Abba's name, which we agreed for me to be known as by those in this part of the country so as not to let anyone know my real identity. With all the problems that Giesell was facing in her family, I didn't want to add to it by letting people know that her first husband was now one of those afflicted with tzara'at. I mentioned that I had been with David and the group at an earlier time but had been spending time with family further up in the north country, having just arrived back this morning. I thanked her for her generosity and faithfulness in caring for the sick. I asked her to pass along the same thankfulness to all those people who had done the same.

As time passed and Dorlas became used to me being with David and caring for him and Zeresh, she became more talkative. But this being the first day that we had met, I imagine that she didn't feel too comfortable talking to a stranger, for regardless of what David told me, she did not stay long at all. When she turned around for the trip back to town, I picked up the pot and walked back toward the tent, placing the pot on the fire for it to reheat the meal for us to eat.

David didn't move, and I thought that he might have fallen asleep. I moved the flap aside and went to where Zeresh was lying on his bed. Finding a few bowls on the small table, I took one out and scooped some soup into the bowl, returning to the tent. Huddled under the blanket, Zeresh seemed to be cold. I placed the bowl on the table beside the bed and reached for another blanket to cover him.

Suddenly, I felt fingers on my hand, and looking down, I saw Zeresh reaching up. Looking into his eyes, I saw recognition there. "Gaius, you came back." His speech reminded me of the softness of Mother's voice, and I moved closer in order to hear what he was saying. He moved his head slowly to the side and attempted to push himself up to a sitting position. There was nothing for him to lean against, and sitting straight under his own strength, I believe, would have been too much of a strain on him.

As I sat down on the bed, helping him sit up, I spoke of the soup that had been brought for us, putting an arm around him for support while, with the other hand, reaching out to get a spoonful of soup to feed him. He took a few bites and then lifted his hand to signal that was all that he wanted. Placing the spoon back in the bowl, I asked if he wanted to lie back down, but he shook his head.

We sat there for a few minutes quietly. I still had my arm around him, and he was leaning against me. His eyes were closed, and his mouth appeared to be moving, but there was no sound coming out. Then, he opened his eyes, and one hand reached out to touch mine.

"Gaius, you don't know how many days it has been since I asked Adonai for the chance to speak to you again before I leave this life. I was afraid that I would not have the opportunity to tell you what I have done to you."

First off, this was the first time that I had heard Zeresh mention Adonai. I didn't even know that he was part of our Jewish community. He and Rivkah had been the first people that I had met from the Gerasene district, so I did not know that there were people who believed as we did, living in that area. But I guess that I shouldn't be surprised. There were families whose beliefs were different from my family living in our community, so why wouldn't Jewish families be living in other communities, even in the cities east of the river?

Next, when he spoke of needing to tell me of something that he had done to me, I was extremely puzzled. As I looked at him, his eyes were closed, and I thought that he had fallen asleep. A moment later, I felt him stirring, and he sat up a bit straighter as though he had gotten strength breathed into his body.

"Gaius, I need to tell you that you are here because of me. I am the one who affected you with this terrible disease."

I started to interrupt, but he raised his hand slightly to stop me.

"It was a day very long ago, even before I met Rivkah. I had been visiting relatives that lived in Jerusalem. I had been there a couple of weeks, and at that time, I was returning home. The road that I took was leading to Jericho. It was getting late in the afternoon, and I was hoping to clear the pass before it got dark. I had heard that was not the place to be when the sun went down. I was rushing down the slope and had almost made it through the pass when some robbers came along, beat me, ripped off my clothes, and left me for dead." He stopped for a moment to catch his breath and noticed a look of astonishment on my face.

I had entirely forgotten that event in my life. As Zeresh rested his eyes and his voice for a few moments, I remembered the part that I had in the story.

I, too, had been in Yerushalayim, having come down from Be-it-Anya (Bethany) after visiting with Remah and her new husband, Mathias. They had only been married a short time when Mathias announced that they would be moving to the area around Yerushalayim. He would be studying to become a teacher in the synagogue, and it just made sense that they lived in a place where the focus of the people was on the temple and the rituals of Jewish life. We had been there for three weeks, helping them to get settled in their new home.

It wasn't long before the time that Abba took me down to join the Guard. That year Mother decided that with Delai now becoming a young woman and before my career took me away from the family, us being so near to Yerushalayim of Y'hudah, it would be an excellent time for us to learn more about our ancestry. Now that I think about it, she had also made the trip with Remah, Helgi, and Moreda a few years before they had left home to become wives and mothers. Abba was unable to make the trip with us as he had necessary duties with the Guard that had to be completed in a timely fashion, and no one else was qualified to do them.

After leaving Remah and Mathias to their new life, we spent six months visiting distant family members around the area, and I was able to take in the sights of the great architectural works of Yerushalayim. It was exactly what I had dreamed of doing for many years. But that would not be where my life path would take me.

Once we planned the journey home, Mother and Delai walked along with a group that was heading to Yericho. I was a little way behind them, having to deal with a very stubborn donkey that did not like the road that we had to take. It might have been the load of bundles on his back that he did not like to have to carry. Either way, he was making it a very difficult and slow journey for me.

There were lots of travelers on the road, most of the families hurrying along that very dangerous place as fast as they could. Many passed me as if I were standing still. I noticed a Levite who was hastening down the lane, trying to catch up with his group. I had seen them pass me by a little while prior to that time. A cohen had also passed by, but if I remember correctly, he had gone by just a little while after the group of Levites had come along.

I was suddenly jarred back into the present time. Zeresh was continuing his story about the incidents that surrounded him during that time. He told of the cohen he had noticed and called out for help as he lay there on the ground, beaten and in pain. The man looked his way and then crossed to the other side of the road to pass him by. A few minutes later, a Levite came racing down the path, seeing Zeresh's body on the side of the road, and moved, as the cohen had done, to the other side of the road and continued on his way.

"Gaius, I was about to give up when I looked up and saw a young man leading a donkey down the road. I collected all the strength I had left in me and called out for mercy. *You* were the one who came to rescue me. You cleaned my wounds and dressed them with bandages that you had in one of your bags. Then, you helped me onto the donkey, and we made our way to an inn outside of Jericho. You stayed with me for two days, continuing to clean my wounds and keeping them bandaged. You fed me and cared for me. After that, you told me that you were going to have to leave, but I could stay there until I was well again."

Yes, I knew that after being two days behind Mother and Delai, they would begin to wonder about me. I went to the innkeeper, gave him some of my wages, and asked him to take care of the man that I had brought in. I would return and pay him more if he had to spend extra on caring for the wounded man.

I traveled on to Yericho and met up with Mother at the house of one of her dear friends, who had graciously put them up while they awaited my arrival. After unloading the bundles from the donkey, giving him food, and eating a little for myself, I explained the situation to Mother, mentioning that I had given my word that I would return to pay any outstanding debt that might have occurred since I had left the inn. Arrangements were made for her and Delai to tarry there while I made the trip back to the inn.

The next morning, I made the trip back to the inn and paid for what was needed. I was told that the healing was completed and that the young man had felt well enough to continue his journey home. I had never known the young man's name, and I had never thought I would meet him again. But that same man was now sitting at my side. I saw the tears in his eyes as he spoke of that time in his life.

"When I returned home, I noticed an outbreak on my arm. I was told to go see the cohen at the synagogue. I didn't know what good that would do because the cohen was so old, and people thought that he had lost his wisdom years in the past. I did go and see him, though, and he told me it looked like tzara'at. When I mentioned this to my friends, they laughed and said that now they were positive that the cohen had lost his mind. Why? There had not been a case of tzara'at for years anywhere in our country.

"Being close to my family, I didn't want to take any chances. I made a trip down to Philadelphia, where I met the cohen that was highly respected in the area. A week had already passed by the time I arrived and told him of what the cohen of Gadara had said to me about the rash. After examining the area, he agreed that I was affected by tzara'at. I would need to isolate myself immediately and follow the rules of our people to keep others safe from the disease.

"I am sorry, Gaius. I am the one who caused you to become affected. I am the one who took you away from your family.

"When you first came to camp, I thought that you would recognize me and you would know that I was the reason that you were here, but you never said a word. When you left, I thought that it was the best thing for me since I would never have to tell you. As the months went by, Rivkah told me that I should have mentioned it to you, that it would have given me some relief; it would have been less of a burden that I had to bear along with this disease. She believed that keeping that information from you and inside of myself had begun to eat away at me from within.

"It was then that I knew that Adonai would have to bring you back into my life so that I could let you know the truth. I realized that I didn't have the strength to go around the country looking for you. I wasn't even sure where to start. We knew that you had gone to live close to your sister in K'far-Nachum but weren't sure if you were still there. I promised Rivkah before she died that I would somehow find a way to tell you everything. I spent a lot of time asking Adonai to bring you back here for that very reason. And He did because you are here. I just wish that I had told you sooner so you would know that you have done nothing to deserve what has happened to you. You were just being kind and helping a stranger that was hurt."

I sat there for about twenty minutes with my arm around him. We did not talk, but I knew, and Zeresh knew that things between us were fine. As he moved to lie down on his bed, I spoke,

"Zeresh, you might think that you were the cause of how my life turned out, but I know that you were just the instrument that Adonai was using to get me to this place. I was meant to be here. I am not clear on the reason that I am needed here; still, I know that this is not your fault. My mother used to tell us these words:

'No matter what we do with our days on earth, Adonai controls all things.' His purpose is the reason that I—the reason that you—needed to be here at this time and in this place."

He looked at me with a thoughtful look on his face and said, "You know, Gaius, my mother used to say the same thing to me."

After he had fallen asleep, I stood watching and thinking, about what I do not remember. Soon after that, I turned and took more bowls out to the fire to fill them for David and me.

I stirred up the fire so that the soup in the pot might warm a little so that David and I might be able to enjoy it more. As I pulled open one of my bundles in order to get some bread to go with the soup, I noticed David was awake and watching me. He asked how I was doing, and we spoke of different things while I continued to warm our meal. I told him that I had given Zeresh some of the soup and that he was now resting again.

As we ate, I told him more about the adventures that I had while traveling. I spoke of different sorts of people that I had become acquainted with and some of the festivities that I had watched from a distance.

The days pretty much passed in the same manner. We would awaken, and David and Zeresh would remain at the camp while I did my daily excursions around the woods on the side of the mountain. On my way back down, I would gather wood for the fire. Dorlas, most days, would be the one who brought soup, sometimes bread, and a little fish. She would stay and talk for a while before taking her leave.

About a week after my arrival back at the camp, when I had come back from my walk and the gathering of the wood, I arrived to see David sitting in a chair beside the tree. There was a strange look on his face, and I started wondering what could be the matter.

Noticing a movement of the tent flap, I turned to see Zeresh coming through the opening. His steps were small and hesitant, but he continued until he was able to sit in the other chair that had been brought out from one of the tents and placed outside in order for me to have a place to sit with David during the days when Zeresh was unable to get out of bed. David told me that there were more chairs available, so I went into the tent and brought another one out to the tree. We would all enjoy the time that we could sit and talk with each other.

Both Zeresh and David's facial features were slowly showing more loss due to the severity of the disease, but they were still able to hold conversations with each other as I was busy putting together the meals that had been brought out for us. Before eating, Zeresh would give thanks to Adonai for the healing that had been bestowed on him. He would also give thanks for the food and the kindness that was shown to us by different families in the community, many of whom were not well off but were still willing to share the little that they had that we might have food to eat.

After two weeks of being back in camp and seeing an improvement in the overall strength of Zeresh, I felt that maybe he was beginning to feel better. Since he had let me know about the guilt that he felt about the disease and knowing that I did not place any blame upon him, I believe that was part of the healing that was now taking place inside of him, which in turn, was giving more strength to the outside of him.

One day he took a turn for the worse.

Since he and David had been there the longest, they shared a tent together while my tent was a little distance away but still within shouting distance. I had gone out early that morning to walk the trails and gather wood for the fire. I was close to the point where I turned toward the tents when I saw David hobbling toward me. I asked him what was wrong, and he said that he had been up most of the night tending to Zeresh. He had begun running a fever and was delirious, ranting and raving about something from his past.

As we walked back into camp and I dropped the wood on the heap that was unused from the previous day, I asked David why he didn't call me; I would have come over and helped care for Zeresh.

He looked at me in disbelief. "Why would you be willing to help him after what he had done to you?"

"David, what are you talking about?"

"I am talking about Zeresh affecting you with tzara'at."

"How did you find out about it?"

"I found out this morning when Zeresh was rambling on about what had happened on the trip from Jerusalem to Jericho. Why wouldn't you tell me about this situation? I thought that we were able to tell each other anything."

Wearily, I reached up and rubbed my neck with my hand. "I figured it wasn't my story to tell. It was Zeresh that had been robbed and beaten nearly to death. He was the one who cried out for mercy as people would walk right past him without any thought of his well-being. I just happened to be in the right place at the right time."

"I do not know why you are thinking the way that you are." David pointed in the direction of the tent. "In there lies a man that gave you a disease that has separated you from your wife, from your family, and from your career. Why would you be willing to help him? How can you forgive him for all that he has done to you?"

I sat down on a rock next to the fire and began adding sticks in order to begin the warming of the morning meal. And for a few moments, David paced around the best that he could, still going on about the fact that he would not be able to care for anyone who had affected him with a disease. But the way that he was ranting about the situation that he had just become aware of led me to believe that this was not the only thing that was causing all this anger. There had to be something more bothering him. Something that I felt he wanted to talk about yet was unable to bring it up in a conversation. Finally, I asked him to sit down. As he did, I spoke,

"What if you had been the one who affected Zeresh or me? Would you not have accepted our help? Or if I had been the person with the rash that had come in contact with you? If we don't help ourselves and each other, who will?

"Does it really matter how things happened? We can't spend our days blaming people for the situations that we find ourselves in. What happened in the past has the ability to inhabit our thoughts so much that we cannot move past them. We become stuck in time, and after a while, that reasoning gets to the point where it runs our very lives; it takes over our every waking moment. We become bitter and want to shut out the very people who want to help us. If we are not careful, all that we feel leads to hostility toward the people around us, those people who are not affected and are going on with their normal lives. We wonder, 'Why me and not them?' We ask ourselves what we could have possibly done to deserve this while others in town go to celebrations with family and friends. They have jobs and don't have to call out 'unclean' every time they get close to someone. You, Zeresh, and I could spend our days thinking thoughts like that, but it is just a vicious circle that will keep us from everything else.

"Life is too short for any thoughts of the past narrating how I live my life. I see this time as an unexpected trip that I can take, not only by walking the countryside but also by reflecting on the years gone by and speculating what is coming in the future."

David spoke up, his voice flat, "We have no future. All we have to look forward to is someone coming around to roll our bodies in a burial cloth and putting us in the ground."

"David, that is the bitterness that is talking. I know that since you lost Tirtzah, you have been hurting greatly. I understand there was more you were expecting from your life. Yet there is so much more left to do and to see."

"You are probably right, Gaius. Maybe it is the bitterness that is talking, but there are things that have happened in the past that I have never told anyone. I believe after what I have gone through, I am allowed to be bitter." He sat for a moment with a stick in his hand, tracing a circle in the dirt. Not wanting to push, I waited until he was ready to speak.

"I was born in the town of Nain. My mother left when I was young, and there are only a few things that I can remember about her. My father never recovered from what he considered to be a betrayal. I don't know anything about the situation except for what he told me, which was not much at all. But the way that he dealt with me after she left removes any doubt in my mind about who he thought was responsible for the upheaval in his life. For years, he never came right out and said the words; he would always say, 'She did this' or 'Your mother is why this is happening to me.'

"That went on for a few years in which he became so obsessed with why things would always go wrong, why all that he did never came out the way that he expected. And that began to rub off on me. I started having thoughts of my own about how my mother could go and leave me alone with this man that only thought of himself. Did she love me? Was I not her son? How could any mother find any justification within herself to abandon her own child? I never asked for any of this, yet here I was with no mother and a father that didn't care whether I was in his life or not.

"Father began to drink wine. He had gotten a job in a vineyard a few months before, and I guess that he just began sampling what he was making. For years it went on and eventually got worse. He could not do his job; he could not take care of me, yet through it all, he never stopped complaining about how my mother had wrecked his life. Then, one day, after he had been drinking for what seemed to be an entire week, it slipped out. He actually spoke the words while staring straight at me, 'I blame you for all of this!' After that, I could not look at him without being reminded of those words.

"Not very long after that, he died, and I was left alone. I was about twelve at the time and did not know what I was going to do. We had never been close to anyone in town, and I did not know of any family members who had ever visited. We had never made trips to see anyone. I even thought to myself, *If my father is the way he is with me, will his family be any different? Will they put the blame for all of this on my mother or me?*

"And as for my mother, I didn't know anything about her, whether she was still alive. Would she want to see me after all these years? Did she have any family? Would I want to find her, and if it were possible to locate her, how would I react when seeing her, knowing what I had gone through after she had left? There were so many questions that went through my mind, and I could not find any answers. I asked around town, but no one remembered my mother's name, who her family was, or from which town she had come. So, the thought that I could be reunited with my mother, or anyone else in her family, had to be dropped from my mind.

"For months, I lived on the edge of town and would beg for bread or anything to eat from strangers that knew nothing about my life. I began to lose any belief, if I ever had any, in mankind. Constantly, I had seen the looks of people as they walked by, wondering why I was there. Some of them even asked me why I wasn't looking for some kind of work that I could do in order to support myself. I stayed there for almost a year and never got much from anyone, so I decided to begin a new life, hoping that things would change for me.

"There was a band of travelers that came through from the south, heading to the northland, and I asked if I could join their group. I was welcomed, and for the time of the trip, I enjoyed the company of people who did not care how I came to be there or why I was leaving town. I had plenty to eat and felt comfortable around people for the first time in my life.

"We came to the town of Nazareth, and I decided to stay there. The travelers continued on. I found a place to belong in Nazareth. It took a while since I was not considered Jewish, for they made up a lot of the townspeople, but there I found peace.

"I guess that I just needed to get away from the memories that I had in Nain; I really don't know. I do know that after I arrived, I felt like I was finally home. I found a man that was willing to teach me a trade while I worked in his shop for food and shelter. He had a nice family; a young wife and a young son. Then, there were some older children who were married and out on their own. They must have been from his first marriage. Anyway, Joseph taught me a lot about carpentry, and his family gave me great support during the time that I was there. After about five years, I felt as if I had learned enough, and after saying my goodbyes, I left and went further north to Cana. It was never quite the same, but I made a living and found Tirtzah. We had a great but short time together. And you know the rest of the story."

It took a few minutes to take in all that I had just heard from my friend, and I gathered my thoughts on what I might be able to say that would help him.

"David, when I was growing up, I often wondered what made my Abba the way that he was throughout his life. We were not close to anyone on his side of the family; in fact, Remah and Helgi were the only ones that I knew of that had actually met any of his family. They were so young that they were not able to remember what the parents of Abba were like. All that we knew was what Mother told us when we were old enough to understand.

"Abba's mother had died when he was quite young, and I guess that his father became like your father did when he was left alone to raise a child. He did the best that he could for a few years and then took another wife so that he could have some help. Then, they began to have a family of their own, which took the focus off of Phinah and gave more attention to the younger children. Abba watched his father with them and began to wonder why his father was never the same with him as with the other children.

"Abba did not really have a role model while he was young. Someone who would teach him how to be a father to his children. But my mother would always tell him that he had the strength inside of him that would enable him to be the best that he could be and that we, as his children, would know that he loved us. He would be able to be an example to us.

"Maybe that is why your father was the way he was after your mother left. He did not know that he had the ability inside of him to be the father that he needed to be for you. There is really no way for us to know why he became the way he did. It could have been that it was what he had gone through when he was younger, and he believed that it was the normal reaction to life. Without someone to teach him, he did not know how to be a father to you.

"David, I think that you have done a great job with overcoming what had been the life in which you grew up. All the challenges that you had to face have helped you to become the man that you are today. I don't think that anyone could have accomplished more than you have. You put the past with your father behind you. You left a town where you were a nobody, where no one was willing to help you, and you found your own way through the life that you have been given. The looks that people gave you, their telling you to work in order to support yourself, might have bothered you at the time. As you left that place, you made a deliberate decision that you were not going to let that bring you down to the point where you could not rise. You took your life into your own hands and found a place where you could belong. You found people who were able to show you what family really means.

"I am not saying that all things are rosy every day of your life. There are times when brothers get on the nerves of their sisters and times of disagreements. Fighting is a way of letting one person know that you are different from who they are; we cannot all be the same. That would make the world a boring place if we were. Yet, even after fighting with one person on one day, the very next day, you might find out that there are more things that you have in common than those on which you disagree.

"You overcame the discord in the life that you had with your father, continuing to move on and learn a skill that would allow you to care for Tirtzah. You had quite a few wonderful years with her and…."

David broke in, "And then, I lost her. I lost the love of my life because of a disease that, for some reason, picked us to inhabit. Gaius, for many nights, I would lay beside Tirtzah, looking up into the night sky and wondering, why us? Why would we be the ones selected for this problem to occur in our lives? Why could we not have been the couple that lived out their entire lives in peace with each other and our neighbors? Why are we the ones that will not have a family to care for us when we get older?

"Gaius, I don't see any point to it. Our fate has been written in the stars; there is no help for us. There is no hope."

"You're wrong, David. There is always hope. You just have to believe. You have to believe that there is a reason for *all* of your life. For the things that you had to go through as you were a child, the things that you have gone through from that point to this.

"I know that there has to be a reason for this disease that has taken over so much of our bodies. We have to be willing to wait and learn that reason. And you should remember that you have the family that you were born into, just as now you have a different family in this life that you can rely on to help you when you need them. You just have to look around and be open to the people as they become aware that you need their help. You need to be willing to stretch out your arms and welcome those of us that will care for you, helping you as much as we can in any way that we can."

For a few minutes, David sat there silently, shaking his head while looking at the fire. I continued on with the preparations for our meal. A while later, David rose from the rock and went into the tent. Within a couple of moments, he emerged with news that Zeresh's fever had broken and he was sleeping. I was the one who said thanks that day.

About a month later, with David and me both caring for Zeresh, he was able to stand on his own and walk out of the tent to en- joy a day in the sunlight. We were soon to be heading into the rainy season, and although we like to watch it fall and listen to the drops hitting the tents when we were trying to sleep, the thought of trudging through the mud, trying to find enough dry wood to make fires through the day was not my idea of a great time. As part of my morning routine, after my training was done, I began to gather up firewood and bring it into camp. I stacked it in what remained of the tent of our silent acquaintance, Yo'ed. When the rains did begin, at least we would have a good supply of wood that was dry, and I would not have to use all my energy walking up the mountain searching for wood that could be used for cooking and keeping us warm.

Later that morning, Dorlas came on her regular visit. With her, she brought news of a group of young carpenters who were traveling the countryside and helping put up shelters and building furniture for those who needed them. She had spoken to her husband, as did some of the other women who helped her in their endeavor to keep food and water coming out to us. They had, in turn, approached the council of the town, who agreed to ask the group to come our way and set up some rooms for us. It wouldn't be anything fancy, but it would be better than just living in a tent. They should be arriving within a week.

We could not express our thankfulness enough, and Dorlas was glowing with great honor as she left, knowing that she had done a good thing to help her neighbors. I wondered exactly how many of the townspeople would agree that building permanent shelters for those who were afflicted with tzara'at was such a good thing. Probably not many because that would make them realize that we were here to stay. As long as we just lived in tents, we were able to leave whenever we wanted. But, with a shelter to keep us dry, why would we ever want to leave?

Before she left for the day, however, Dorla was sitting across from Zeresh, telling him about the happenings around town. Since she knew that Rivkah had relatives that lived in town and throughout the countryside, she often brought news of Rivkah's people; she spoke of the celebrations in regard to children born in the area and that there were a few deaths of the elderly. There were also men of high rankings throughout the town that were being promoted, and the rich were getting richer while there were others traveling to other parts of the country trying to find work that they could do just to feed their families.

Then she spoke of "some harlot" that people were talking

about and how she had been married four times already and was now involved with another man. It seems like the woman had been trying for years to do anything she could in order to get to a higher place in society. The stories that were being told around town were too numerous to tell, and the details, well, they were not repeated by anyone with even the slightest of good upbringing!

By the way she said those words, I realized that they had to be very harsh words that were being repeated about this woman and the life that she was leading. But in my heart and mind, I knew exactly to whom Dorlas was referring before any name was ever spoken.

I quietly walked away from the group and went out into the forest. I sat on a log far out of sight of the camp and tried my best to figure out what went wrong. Why was Giesell acting in this manner? I knew from our childhood that she did want to become someone in high society, one whom others would look upon and dream about becoming just like her someday. But to go about it in this manner was not the way to accomplish her desire. For a while, I just sat there, wondering what I could do to help her.

I came up with nothing.

When I returned to camp, Dorlas had left for town, and David was stoking the fire in order to heat the meal that had been brought for the day. I moved over beside him, beginning to help with the preparations.

After we had eaten, Zeresh moved into the tent to rest. David and I took a small amount of water in order to clean the bowls that we had just used. Then, we sat down, and he spoke first,

"I am sorry that you had to hear the news of Giesell in that manner. Zeresh and I both know that you didn't want it to be known around town that you were her husband. After being here all these months, you know that we cannot say anything to stop Dorlas from speaking on any subject without raising questions in her mind as to why."

"Thank you, David. I know that it is hard for things to remain secret for such a long time. I am glad, for Giesell's sake, that we have been able to keep this one from the people of the town. I didn't realize that she had gotten such a bad name for herself. I thought that she would have just gotten remarried, begun raising a family, and be satisfied with what she had received."

I don't recall how long it was that we sat there in silence; it couldn't have been too long. Suddenly, Zeresh came out of the tent like he had the energy of a ten-year-old, with the enthusiasm to match.

"I know what we should do. We should pack up and go to K'far-Nachum. Gaius, it has been some time since you have been to see your mother, and Moreda must have had her baby by now. It is quite a distance, but we can do it. You can show us the ways that you have traveled before, and we can see all the great sights of which you have spoken."

I looked at David, and he looked at me. We started laughing and talking about the great plan that was now laid before us. It was what we all needed, something to get our minds off of what was heard in the camp today. Yes, it would take time to get there, especially since Zeresh had recently been ill. But we had decided that if he was up for the trip, so were we.

When the boys came a little later with the water for our use throughout the night and the next day, we explained to them that this would not be necessary to continue. David asked them to please take the message to Dorlas, and she, in turn, could let the others know that we would be away from camp for a while. We would bring word to her when we arrived back from our trip.

We spent a few hours resting, then rose and packed up our belongings. We figured that we would take one tent as we would need shelter for when the rains came. I told of some caves that I had seen in the mountains that would also be good for getting out of the rain.

Before the sun came over the horizon, we were on our way, with excitement building inside of me with every step. It would be great to see my mother again!

David and Zeresh continued losing more of their ability for everyday activities, and I was beginning to show more symptoms of the effects of the disease that had taken over our bodies. Somedays, I wondered how any of us made it through the day's travel. We had often talked about what we would be going through when we came to the end of our journey of life, but I didn't think that we actually knew how difficult it would be for any of us. For this moment in time, I just wanted to survive the journey that we were facing in order for us to reach our destination.

It was slow going, but Zeresh showed great resolve to make it as far as he could every day. David and I questioned him constantly about whether he could continue. Sometimes, I was the one who wanted to stop and rest more than he did, yet we persevered. There were one or two days, though, when we all overdid our traveling abilities and ended up camping for three days trying to regain our strength. Even though I wanted to get to see my mother as soon as I could, our bodies would only take so much. Eventually, we arrived and set up our tent along the outskirts of an already existing small colony of those affected with tzara'at.

As we settled in, we found that they had just lost about half of the ones who were living there. Most of them just gave up and stopped eating, withering away before the eyes of the others who constantly wondered why they had to go through all the pain.

There were only seven people left when we came into the camp. They welcomed us and even helped us set up our tent.

Our newly found friends, most of whom were from the area and had been camping together for some time, introduced themselves as we got settled. Kalev, Hevel, Elah, and Sha'ul had been there the longest; Asha, Manal, and Akan, for about two years. They were part of what had been a big colony of those affected with the disease and were trying to cope the best that they could. Hevel mentioned that at one time, just after he had arrived, there were twenty-two persons who had lived in the camp. After we had been there for a couple of days and we were feeling comfortable enough, we left Zeresh at the tent and took off to see my mother.

She was overjoyed when she came to the doorway after Moreda had called to her as we arrived at the edge of the yard. I introduced David to Moreda, and she motioned for us to come into the yard. We sat on the ground. Moreda brought cups of water along with bread and fish that they had readied for the midday meal.

While we ate, they spoke of things that had been happening in town and the surrounding countryside. We spoke of the three of us that had just made the trip from Sh'khem and had set up our residence at the camp on the south side of town.

Mother was thriving, helping around the house and being just as helpful in the community. In fact, she began speaking about how she and some of the women in town, who were her closest friends, would come out to the camp and see how they could aid those who needed it most.

We had been there quite a while when David mentioned that we should get back to camp to see how Zeresh was coping with being alone with the rest of our newly found colony. Moreda packed up some food for us to take back, and Mother mentioned that we would see her tomorrow. She would bring her friends and would be making arrangements for daily visits. They would be delighted to see how they could assist in supporting us in any way that they could.

We traveled back to camp and set the food before everyone. Zeresh, as usual, offered up thanks for the sustenance that had been provided and the blessings that had been bestowed upon us all. A few minutes had passed when one of the men noticed that two figures were coming down the road. As they got closer, I could make out two young men carrying a water vessel between them. They stopped before they got to the tent and called out that they were told to bring this out for us to have fresh water. I knew that Mother had already begun her service for us.

We all rested well that night, with nourishment that many of those men had not received in a long time.

True to her word, Mother came marching down the road toward the camp with a few of her friends early the next morning. They took one look around and decided that what the camp had been accustomed to was no longer acceptable. They would be finding those in the community who would be willing to make new tents for us. The carpenters of the town would supply us with chairs so that we would have places to sit, and there would be beds so that we no longer had to sleep on the ground.

Within a week, the camp that we were now a part of was a lot different than the one that we had found when we came to town. Each of the men had a bed, not just a mat on the ground, and there was a long table brought over for our meals. There were two lean-to shelters set up and new tents that would keep us out of the elements when needed. A few benches and stools were also supplied by builders from around town. They also brought in a few extras that could be set apart from the tents for those people of town who wanted to stay and visit for a time.

Mother had indeed proven that she could get people to help support those of us who could not provide on our own. One of the women suggested that we take branches and move the dirt as one would do around the house; otherwise, the dirt would become hardened and feel like stone. The women unpacked bowls and utensils that could be left for our meals, along with a big pot that would be replenished daily for as long as there was someone in the camp who needed to be fed. Soon after the food was unpacked, the women and workers left to return to their families.

At the end of the day, we had a big fire in order to rid ourselves of all the old materials that had been used for tents and mats, which seemed to usher in a new beginning for us all.

The following day, Mother came early with our food for the day. After emptying it into the pot that sat on the stone, she walked away a few steps, turned, and motioned to me that she needed to speak to me. The day that David and I had been to Moreda's house, I felt like there was something that my mother had wanted to speak of but didn't feel comfortable bringing it up in front of Moreda or David. And with all the changes that had been made throughout the camp, there had been no time until then for the subject to be approached. As we were sitting apart from the group, Mother spoke of things that had happened before I returned.

Moreda and Shim'on were still childless as the baby did not survive. Moreda had taken it hard but was learning to cope with the loss that was part of life itself. Another change that had come to impact the family was that Shim'on was not with the fishing crew any longer.

Earlier that year, at Pentecost, Shim'on had traveled with his brother, Andrew, to Yerushalayim. While there, they met up with someone that they said was the Mashiach (Deliverer—Messiah). He seemed to be a great teacher and had done some miraculous signs around the country.

Shim'on had returned home for a while, but now he was out traveling the countryside with this teacher along with Andrew, Yochanan (John), and Ya'akov (James), both bars of Zavdai (Zebedee), the fisherman. They would stop by every now and then to make sure that things were going well with Moreda and the other families. Zavdai and his crew continue to help supply fish and support the family.

This time, they had been gone for a while. Word had come back to Moreda that they were in Sh'khem for a couple of days and then went on to the Galil. They were hoping that he would stop by the house, maybe even stay for a few days but were not sure when or if that would happen.

During the time that we had been in that discussion, a couple of young men came with the daily water to fill our vessels. Mother told me that a few of the women from the neighborhood had offered to give their sons the job of bringing water for us. They were using us as examples of what the outcome would be if they were to disobey their parents or the rabbi. While Mother did not condone the use of this tactic in her own life or the life of her family, she was not one of these women that would declare it to be off limits for others. They would keep their families in check the way that they thought was best, and she, in turn, would do the same with her family.

She decided to leave with the young men as they were returning to town. Moreda did not like her traveling the roads alone all the time. She stated that she would be back tomorrow with more food and provisions for the camp.

We were three weeks into the stay outside of K'far-Nachum, going through our early morning rituals, when I noticed a figure walking down the road. It was not my mother or any of her friends, as this person was walking faster than the older women could travel, especially those who might be carrying a day's worth of provisions for the camp. Still, the movement of that person that I saw looked familiar.

As the figure moved closer and I could see more clearly, I recognized Giesell. I was speechless. After all this time, I would not have believed that I would ever see her again. I moved toward her, putting a small distance between the rest of the camp and us. When she saw me coming, she lifted her hand and waved to me. We found a couple of boulders spaced far enough apart to keep her safe, but also, as we talked, we would be able to hear each other.

"Hello, Gaius; it is good to see you again. I hope that you don't mind that I came here to talk to you."

I wondered aloud, "How did you know where to find me?"

As she settled on the rock, she explained, "I had gone out to the camp and found that it was deserted. As I walked back, I met a woman who had been one of those who had been supplying food to the group. She spoke of her friend, Dorlas, who had been the one who had begun helping out the ones who were afflicted with tzara'at. She told me where I could find her. When I returned to town, I went to meet with Dorlas to explain the reason that I needed to know if she knew where the men that once lived out in the camp were living now. At first, she did not want to give out the information; but after hearing what I had to say, she let me know that one of the men, David, had sent word to her that they were going to move to K'far-Nachum.

"I went back home, telling my mother what I was going to do, packed a few things, and found a group of travelers that were coming in this direction. I asked if I could join them for the trip, and they agreed. We have been traveling for some time, much longer than I had planned on taking the trip, but because there were small children who could not travel as quickly or for as long as we could, it took a few extra days." She sat a bit straighter; I guessed that her back was hurting, and she wanted to relieve some of the pain.

I didn't know if she wanted me to ask or if she was going to continue on her own, but I spoke, "Why are you here? Why did you come all this way to see me?"

She rubbed her forehead and reached into a side bag for a water bag, taking a small drink. As she placed the bag on the rock beside her, she began once more with her story, "I wanted to tell you about an encounter that I had with a man whom I think you should meet." Again, she paused, and I waited for her to continue.

"Early one morning, I went to the well to get some water for the day."

I interrupted, "Giesell, why would you be at the well in the morning? Everyone knows that you go in the evening to draw water for the next day."

She blushed and hung her head. "There was too much talk going around town about me, and I could neither face that nor the stares of the women anymore. They did not want to have anything to do with me; they did not want me near their families. I had to find a time that I could be at the well alone. The morning seemed to be the best time to go get water.

"This certain morning, I was not alone. There was a man sitting beside the well who looked to be very tired. I am sure that he had been traveling a great distance, so he would not know about things that were going on around town and in my life. I figured it was safe enough to get water. I was not prepared for the conversation that I was about to have with a stranger. And, Gaius, you are not going to believe it.

"As I lowered the bucket, he asked me if I would give him a drink. By his speech and the way that he looked, I could tell that he was a Jew. You know that I have nothing against the Jews, but it is part of our custom that we, as Samaritans, have nothing to do with the Jews, just as they have nothing to do with us. I told him as much. I said, 'You are a Jew, and I am a Samaritan woman. How can you ask me for a drink?' He answered in the strangest of ways. He said, 'If you knew the gift of God and who it is that asks you for a drink, you would have asked him, and he would have given you living water' (John 4:10). I looked around and saw that he had no way of drawing water from the well. I said to him, 'Sir, you have nothing to draw with, and the well is deep. Where can you get this living water? Are you greater than our father, Jacob, who gave us this well, drank from it himself, as also did his sons, his flocks and herds?'

"He motioned toward the well and answered, 'Everyone who drinks this water will be thirsty again, but whoever drinks the water I give him will never thirst. Indeed, the water I give him will become in him a spring of water welling up to eternal life.' I was amazed at what he was saying."

Giesell broke off the story and looked at me. "Gaius, I had never heard of anyone speaking as this man. All I knew was that I wanted something to quench my thirst, so I said to him, 'Sir, give me this water so I won't get thirsty and have to keep coming here to draw water.' Do you know what he said to me?"

I looked at her and shook my head. She continued with the story of the exchange that she had with this Jewish man that morning beside the well.

"He said, 'Go, call your husband, and then come back.' To which I replied, 'I have no husband.' He again spoke, 'You're right; you don't have a husband! You've had five husbands in the past, and you're not married to the man you're living with now! You've spoken the truth!'

"Knowing that he was not part of our community, I was surprised to hear that he knew so much about me as to know of these past years. I said to him, 'Sir, I can see that you are a prophet. Our fathers worshiped on this mountain, but you Jews claim that the place where we must worship is in Jerusalem.'

"His answer to me, 'Believe me, woman, a time is coming when you will worship the Father neither on this mountain nor in Jerusalem. You Samaritans worship what you do not know; we worship what we do know, for salvation is from the Jews. But the time is coming—indeed, it's here now—when the true worshippers will worship the Father spiritually and truly, for these are the kind of people the Father wants to worship Him. God is Spirit, and worshippers must worship him spiritually and truly.'

"I spoke these words to him. 'I know that the Messiah is coming. When He comes, He will explain everything to us.' And he declared, 'I who speak to you am He.'

"I didn't know what to say. But at that time, a group of men had come up next to him. I left my water jar sitting by the well to go find people in the town to tell them about the man who spoke to me about everything I ever did. I wondered if this could be the Christ. After they had heard what I said to them, they came out to the well to see this man. The men of the town talked him into staying for a while, and he was there for two days. Because of the words that this man spoke while he was there with us, many of the town's people became believers.

"When the group had left to continue on their journey, the men of the town came to talk to me. Their words were: 'We no longer believe just because of what you said; now we have heard for ourselves, and we know that this man really is the Savior of the world.'

"Gaius, do you think that it is possible for this man to be the Christ? Because after many months of being ignored and spoken of behind my back, that was the first time that some of those men dared to look me in the eye, much less speak to me in public."

I sat there and looked at Giesell for a few minutes without speaking. I stood up to stretch my legs as they were hurting from sitting for so long of a time. Returning to the rock, I again sat down, trying to get the thoughts that were racing around in my head to slow down in order for me to comprehend all that I had just heard. I wanted to focus on the encounter with the man at the well and not the facts that Giesell had mentioned about her life over the past few years.

Those years that I had purposely kept away from her in order to keep her safe, the years that I gave to her so that she could have the life that she had desperately wanted. I closed my eyes and took a deep breath, trying to pull something from my heart or from my mind, from which I was not sure. I didn't want the disappointment to be seen in my eyes.

But four husbands after me, and now she was living with a man to whom she was not even married! How was I supposed to handle that? Nothing in the teachings of my mother or the cohen, nor the training that I went through with Abba and the Guard, could have ever prepared me to hear those things about a girl that I had loved for a very long time. She was the one who had moved on from the life that we had known. Why was she telling me all of this?

Was she trying to say that she had changed her ways? That the conversation with the man at the well and throughout those two days that he had spent conversing with the people of Sh'khem had been so overwhelming that it had changed her entire point of view, her entire way of living? What did she want from me?

I guess that I had sat still for such a long time because suddenly I heard a whisper, "Gaius, are you asleep?"

I opened my eyes to see Giesell standing closer but still at a safe distance. She had a worried look on her face, yet when I looked at her again, she smiled.

"Have you heard about what this man has been doing around the country? There have been crowds of people following him. They return to their homes after traveling to other parts of the land, talking about his teachings and how he has been healing sick people. It was said that he had given sight to a blind man, and a lame man is now able to walk. Do you know what this means?"

I wasn't sure what she was saying. My mind had been focused on the news that I had just heard, and now she was asking if I had heard of a man that was teaching the people. Maybe I was tired and had fallen asleep while my mind raced with thoughts of the conversation. It seemed to me that my head was not working right. I could not figure out what point she was trying to make.

"Gaius, this means that we need to go find this man and ask him to heal you. I believe that he can do it. Then, we can be a family again."

I felt my eyes open wide at the words that she had spoken to me. Did she want to be a family again? With me? After all those men that she had been involved with and the different lifestyles to which she had become accustomed within those marriages. I am sure that there were some others that had lifted her into a different "socially acceptable" world than the world that I had been able to provide for her. And after this, being known as a wife of a man who was afflicted with tzara'at, did she really think that this would be opening doors of which she had dreamed all of her life? Maybe it was disbelief that she saw on my face.

"I believe that I know what you are thinking. But Gaius, I have changed.

"I remember the conversations that we had together when we were younger before our fathers came to suggest that we marry. I had always wanted to be someone who was known by everyone in town. I wanted the biggest house on the highest hill so that others would know that a very important person was living there. And for a while, after we had parted, I experienced life in a way that was so much different than what we had together. There were parties and celebrations that I would plan—everything down to the smallest detail so that I knew that people would be talking about it for weeks. It did not turn out to be like that. Oh, maybe for a few hours, they would still remember the happenings of the evening and tell others how much they had enjoyed the time spent at my house.

"People might enjoy the time that they have while together with the group, celebrating. But once they return to their homes, to their lives, the real truth comes out. They criticized every little thing. How this one silly thing went wrong, or why the host would allow his wife to wear that sort of clothing out in public. They would say things like, 'The food tasted terrible; why would anyone have served such a thing to people that they call their friends?' or 'I cannot believe that she actually thought that was acceptable.' No matter how perfect everything turned out to be, there was always at least one person who claimed that they could have done better.

"After a while, I began to feel that I was selfish, thinking only about what I wanted from life and the accolades of the people around me. I wanted to be the person who people always put on a pedestal, one who was always looked up to in every situation as having everything under control. But that was not how I felt when we were together. I felt that I was more important in your eyes, in your life, and I wanted to have that again.

"I remember the times that I would help your mother to ready things for Sabbath. I always enjoyed the time that I would be cleaning beside her. It was just the way that she looked at things, I guess. But I had never had that while I was growing up. Yes, of course, I would help my mother clean the house and the clothes. She would teach me all the things that I needed to make a good wife and mother, just as she was taught by her mother. There was never any enjoyment; it was always just chores that I had to do.

"I finally found out that I do not want that kind of life that I had dreamed of for all those many years. The life of my dreams just doesn't exist. Most of it is because, as humans, we are selfish. We want to be the most important; we want to be the center of our family. But if we are so focused on ourselves, how can we think about doing things for those who are around us? When we stop putting ourselves in the foreground, we can look around us and find out how we can better help those around us who may be hurting in ways that we can understand. We can help them through difficult times. That is what will bring joy into our lives.

"I want to feel the joy in everything that I do. When I would make plans for a celebration or a family gathering, the joy would be there for the first hours, but the joy didn't last, no matter how hard I tried. Therefore, I want to focus more on others rather than myself. I want your mother to again begin teaching me what it means to worship Adonai. And if this man is really the Savior of the world, I think that we need to find him so he can teach us what we need to know about serving Adonai.

"I want the joy that will last for the rest of my life. I know that I had that feeling with you, and I now realize that I could have it again. *We* could have it again! That is why you need to find this man, the Christ, and ask for healing so we can be a family again."

Before I could say anything, I noticed that David had come from the camp.

"Gaius, you have been here for a long time. Did you want to come and have something to eat?"

I had not realized that a good portion of the day had passed while I was there with Giesell. I asked if she would like to have something to eat with us, but she declined, saying that she needed to get to town to make arrangements for a place to stay for a few days. She would return within the next day or two, and we could talk more. I watched her as she walked toward town, with a small amount of relief flooding over me. I needed time to ponder on what she had said and try to decide what I was going to do about all of it.

Gathering with the group for our meal turned out to be what I needed to distract me for a while.

There was something that had been going on between Zeresh, Asha, and Manal. I wasn't quite sure what had happened, but Manal didn't like what the other two had done while he was out of camp. Zeresh and Asha had become close friends over the short time that they had known each other. They always seemed to get into some kind of trouble with the antics that they were constantly playing on the others. It was never harmful, mind you; mainly, it was done to liven the spirits of the rest of the group.

After the meal was completed, Elah, Sha'ul, and Akan took the bowls and utensils to wash them for the next use. Hevel, Zeresh, and Manal walked down the lane to leave the empty water vessels so they could be refilled. David, Kalev, Asha, and I would walk down a little later to get the vessels after the freshwater was brought up by the young men from town.

It really didn't take too much to get into the habit of doing these chores each day, especially when it was your main means of eating and getting water to drink. The way the chores were divided was with the ones who had the most muscle loss and were many times unable to keep themselves balanced, they were the ones that did the washing, which was an easy thing to do. Those who were a little more able to carry the empty vessels would take the two between three men. With the full vessels, it would take two of us to carry each one. Sometimes, I really missed the trips to the well from my younger years. It always brought about thankfulness for those carts and the goats that would help pull those vessels along the paths from house to house. These days, I often wish that we could have a cart and a couple of goats!

Every few days, we would go over to the Galil to wash our bodies and our clothes. We mostly did that in the heat of the day so as not to notice the coldness of the water. And when the weather did turn cold, we didn't even think about the need to get clean. I now know that it was a good thing that we lived mostly outdoors. For if we had been cooped up for weeks without being cleaned, the smell would have been terrible.

As we prepared for the night, David and Zeresh asked me about Giesell. They had gotten the impression that she may have been my wife even though that was the first time they had ever seen her. I told them, yes, it was her. Zeresh stated that they would be there when and if I was ready to talk. I thanked them and turned over toward the tent wall. I lay there motionless as I heard whispers from the other two. Eventually, they went to sleep. But sleep would prove a bit more difficult for me.

The next day, Giesell came again to talk. I hadn't really made any decisions on what I needed or wanted to do. I tried not to think about the life that Giesell had been living and found that in itself was a very hard thing to do. For some reason, doubt kept creeping into my mind. How could I be sure that these things would never happen again? Would I be able to be a husband to someone who had been with other men, living with them and using them for one reason? That reason was to get ahead in society and to have a house on the other side of town. Had she really changed? Was she going to focus on others rather than herself? Would she really be happy with me, as we were before, knowing that we might not make it any further?

But this was only a possibility if this man, the Christ, could heal me of the tzara'at that plagued my body. I mean, Giesell had mentioned hearing about the sick being cured, the blind given back their sight, and the lame becoming able to walk. Not once was the story told of Christ being able to cure someone of tzara'at. Maybe this disease was more than he could cure. At the point that I was at the time, I believed that I might be beyond saving.

I had never heard of tzara'at affecting a person's brain, albeit on that day, the conversation that I had with Giesell; besides one piece of information that she spoke of before she left, I have yet to recall what was spoken between us. The one thing that I do re-member, she told me that soon after the visitation of the man, the Christ as she called him, was the fact that her father had died.

Giesell left for town about the same time that David, Asha, Kalev, and I headed down to bring water back to camp. The rest of the day and into the night, I stayed in the tent, lying on my back, looking up but seeing nothing.

The next morning, as I readied myself to go for my morning run, I felt a bit more like myself. I enjoyed the fresh wind on my face as I traversed the hillside, running around the area for a while, and then started back down toward the camp. As I was finishing the last leg of my run, I saw Zeresh trying to hurry toward me. I came to stop in front of him and could tell by the look on his face that something was wrong.

"Gaius, we just received word from Samuel that your mother has become ill. He was not sure of the cause but was told to let you know that she has a fever. There was not too much that he could tell us."

I leaned over, placing my hands on my knees, trying to catch my breath. In between gasps, I managed to ask how long she had been sick and was told that the fever had come upon her a few days ago. I sat down to rest, thinking that I would walk over to Moreda's house and see for myself how Mother was doing; while seeing if there was a need for a physician to be called in or if this was something that would go away on its own.

Just a while later, I was walking up the lane toward town. Upon arrival at the house, I called Moreda through the door and waited for her to come out. As she appeared, she had a smile on her face. I wondered why, but it was at that instant that she began to speak,

"Gaius, I am glad that you are here. We have some good news that I need to share with you."

"I hope that the good news is that Mother is feeling better."

She motioned for me to sit down, and sat down across from me, then continued with the conversation. "When I sent word around to the ladies that helped Mother take the provisions out to your camp, I didn't realize that all of this was going to happen. I just wish that you could have been here. You would not have believed it. In fact, I didn't believe it, and *I was* here."

In all my memories of our days growing up, I had never heard Moreda sound more confusing; she wasn't making any sense to me. She had always been one of the two, along with our other sister, Remah, to be the most levelheaded of our family. I guess that she had gotten that from Mother, who was the one who could spread calm through the most difficult of circumstances. As I looked at my sister now, I saw a much different person. What was this that she thought I would not have believed had happened?

She was smiling; her foot was tapping on the dirt, and there was joy in her eyes that had been gone for quite a while. I wasn't sure if she wanted me to ask again about what happened to Mother, but as I was preparing to do so, she spoke,

"Gaius, yesterday about midday, Shim'on had come into the house with the group of men with whom he had been traveling. As he entered, I noticed a crowd of people coming down the path toward the house, but I couldn't understand why. Then I saw him. The man that Shim'on had been mentioning to us. I wasn't sure what to do, but I spoke out, saying that Mother was sick with a fever and that it might be best if everyone just stayed outside so as not to become affected with whatever caused the fever. The man Shim'on had called the Rabbi ignored what I was saying and went over to where Mother was lying. He reached out and touched her hand. In that instant, the fever left her. She got up and started helping me with bringing out food so that he might have dinner with us."

She leaned a little way toward me and spoke in a softer tone, "The Rabbi had given Shim'on a new name. He calls him 'Kefa' (Peter), which means 'rock.' I am not sure what that will mean in the days to come, but Shim'on, I mean Peter, does seem to be more solid in his thinking and his actions. When the others had gone out of the house, Peter told me about the healing that they had just witnessed. It was a man that was afflicted with tzara'at. He had come up within a few feet of the crowd, speaking the word 'unclean,' and of course, the crowd started backing away. But the Rabbi walked right up to him, touched him, and healed him from the tzara'at. And I know that he would be willing to do that for you. I believe that he could do that for you."

At that moment, I heard a voice behind me, "I just heard about your mother, Moreda. I wanted to come to see what I could do for her and you."

Moreda looked beyond me and stood to her feet. "What are you doing here?"

I stood up and turned to see Giesell standing at the edge of the yard.

"As I said, I wanted to see what I could do for you and your mother."

Moreda, I could tell, was becoming confused. Then, a figure appeared at the door.

Mother spoke with her usual calming voice, "I am doing well, Giesell. I thank you for being concerned about me." She turned to me, "I am glad to see you, Gaius. I have been missing you for the last few days." Then, she spoke to Moreda, "Let us go and prepare food for our guests. We have a lot to discuss."

Giesell asked to be included in the preparation, and Mother stated that she would not have it any other way. I stayed in the yard, wondering what might be going on inside the house, yet knowing that Mother, in all her wisdom, had things under control.

Minutes later, they were sitting at the table after bringing food out for me. Mother gave thanks to Adonai for the provisions, for the healing, and for the reunion of the family.

As we ate, the conversation turned to the Rabbi and all the reports about what he was doing all over the country. There were healings of very sick people, more stories of blind and lame being made whole again. But much more than that, the belief that was being felt about this man, Yeshua (Jesus), being the Mashiach. The one who was going to deliver the people of Isra'el into the kingdom that had been promised by Adonai.

After the topic had been exhausted, they turned to the conversation that Peter had with Moreda about the healing of the man afflicted with tzara'at and why it was in my best interest to go and find Yeshua so that He could heal me and I could once more come back to my family.

Do you know what it is like to have three women focused on the many reasons why you should do exactly what they say? Well, it is not a pretty sight! I thought it was bad with just one of them, but with all of them in agreement that I should go and find Yeshua in order to be healed, I didn't stand a chance.

They went on for hours trying to get me to see reason, or at least that is what I wanted them to believe. I had made up my mind from the moment Moreda first mentioned to me about the healing of the man that I was going to travel as far as I needed to go to find Yeshua and ask Him to heal me. I no longer wanted to be separated from my family by a disease that could be cured. I wanted to come home again!

CHAPTER THREE

After leaving Moreda's house and returning to camp, it was rather late, and most everyone had gone to rest for the night. As I was exhausted from the walk both into town and back to camp, not to mention the mental draining of all that "woman talk" that I had to endure, I just wanted to rest. Tomorrow would be a good enough time to get started on a new adventure.

The hustling of the men around the camp early the next morning was enough to wake me, but the thought of getting out and moving around to help was a thought I did not want to face for another few minutes. I groaned and rolled over, trying to use the blanket to cover my head and drown out the sound of all that activity that was going on around me. After a few minutes of no relief, I gave up and pulled myself up on my feet.

Zeresh and Asha had already gotten under Manal's skin about something they did or perhaps didn't do. With them, it was hard to know, and after a while, you just got used to all the bickering back and forth that went on between the three. This morning, I tuned them out and went to find David and Kalev.

They were overjoyed to hear that my mother was healthy and back on her feet. They sat in awe as I described the scene as Moreda had spoken about it. I could see great interest in their eyes when the discussion turned to leaving this place to locate this man for healing.

Kalev, along with David, agreed that we should tell everyone, then we could pack up and be on our way in a few hours. After all, if the man, this Yeshua, was powerful enough to heal one, then surely, he was capable of healing all.

I sat in silence, stunned by what I was hearing. Of course, I wanted them all to receive the healing as much as I did for myself. But did they realize how difficult it would be traveling around the countryside with ten men, all in different stages of this dreadful disease? It was hard enough when David, Zeresh, and I had come up from Sh'khem to K'far-Nachum. It had seemed to take us forever to move through the mountains. I mentioned as much to the two men sitting with me. They saw it as a hindrance to be overcome in order to achieve something far more gratifying than a little inconvenience. I just hoped that they would remember that it was me who brought up the possibility of disappointment if, or when, we could not find healing.

As I spoke, I noticed the two figures of Giesell and my mother coming up the path. They stopped at a distance, and I introduced Giesell to David and Kalev. Since Mother had been coming to the camp all this time, she stated that she was glad to be able to see them again after being away for a while. The men, in turn, told her that they were glad that she had made a full recovery from the fever and had the strength to make the trip out to see us. Mother smiled at them both, thanking them, and then began to speak of the reason that they had made the trip.

"I know that you would like to know which way Yeshua was traveling. Peter had brought news to Moreda that the group would be leaving for the other side of the lake."

Kalev turned to me and said, "See, Gaius, this is a sign! The other side of the lake. Everyone knows that it is not as hilly as it is on this side of the lake. There is a lot of flat land throughout the country, with only a few hills. We will be able to find Yeshua in no time."

David spoke to Mother and Giesell, mentioning to them that they thought it would be best if the whole group made the journey together. We were going to discuss it with the others and start packing a few belongings.

"Gaius, that would be nice. You will have company on your travels this time. I am sure that you will be able to catch up with them in the territory of the Gadarenes," Giesell said with confidence. "After all, they are being followed by a larger group than what you are going to have with you. I know that you will be able to meet up with them soon."

Oh, the faith that my mother and Giesell had in this group of ours was so much greater compared to mine, which, I believe, was as small as a grain of sand. And after speaking to them at great lengths, I began to feel that I was right. But finally, it was decided that since the group had been together for this long, we would all pull together to make sure that all of us were there when we met Yeshua.

Mother and Giesell left for town, promising to meet us at the seaside before we left on our journey. There was a flurry of activity as we gathered things for our trip. Leaving the tents where they stood, we, as a group, headed toward the Galil.

Moreda, it seemed, had talked Zavdai, Peter's partner in the fishing business, into letting us have one of his older boats to get across the Galil. A boat that was not being used to take the fishing crews out but one that was still seaworthy and able to hold the entire group of ten men. It would be what we needed to make it to the other side. When we were finished with the boat, it could be used as firewood since it would be considered unclean once it was used by us affected with the disease.

Mother and Giesell had brought along provisions for our trip and were sure that once we reached our destination, there would be others that would help us until we were able to do things on our own again.

Well, it didn't turn out to be that simple. Akan and Hevel were the only two that had ever been in a boat. They did a quick lesson on how the rowing would be repeated. Sha'ul and Elah didn't have enough strength to even help with the rowing. David sat beside Akan and helped him with one oar. Hevel and Zeresh together steered the boat while Kalev and Manal were together on another oar. Asha and I each had oars of our own.

As we crossed the lake, I sat and wondered what I had gotten myself into and how much different my life was from what I had imagined when I was younger. You know, sometimes, when you're doing something that doesn't take too much concentration, your thoughts begin to drift back to a time in your life when things were much simpler. You realize what is expected of you, but you also know the dreams that you have for a different life. In none of my dreams did I ever see myself rowing a boat across the lake during the nighttime hours when all normal people were sleeping. But then, of course, I never dreamed that I would have to deal with any dreaded disease either.

I remember noticing there were a few fishing boats in the distance, but as we steadily kept our boat going across the water, those boats seemed to vanish. Akan continued helping with the rowing as long as he could. But soon, I noticed that David was struggling to row on his own as Akan was lying on the bottom of the boat resting. I don't blame him; it was late, and we had all been on the move the entire day. Hevel and Zeresh had guided the boat at a small angle, and we found ourselves on the northern end of the lake. It was a spot where we could pull toward the shore, anchor the boat, and get some rest. We would continue the journey when the sun rose in the sky.

It didn't seem that we had laid on the ground for very long at all before we felt the sun on our skin, and hearing the lapping of the water against the boat, we woke from our sleep.

Hevel suggested that we row along the shoreline to the south until we came to the Gadarene's territory. There we could moor the boat and continue on foot to where we could find Yeshua. After a few bits of food that had been provided by my mother, we again boarded the boat and began to row.

We rowed for a few hours. Every now and again, we called out when we saw men readying their boats or bringing their catch into shore, asking if they had seen this group that was following Yeshua. From some, we received only stares; others called out that they had seen them the day before and they were heading south. We continued on with our quest to find Yeshua.

Finally, about midday, we were told that the group that we were seeking was just a little further up the road toward the river. We brought our boat ashore and began to walk. We didn't get too far until Sha'ul and Akan had to rest. We sat for a while, ate a little, and listened to Hevel and Manal speaking of what they were going to do once they were healed. They imagined great homecomings with their families.

As we started our walk again, the talk of getting back to families and the lives that we had left behind brought energy to everyone. It seemed that we were moving faster and with fewer rest breaks. I smiled to myself and thought that just maybe we would be able to find the group that was following Yeshua. And then, the healing would begin!

When we came into town, we noticed that there was quite a stir among the inhabitants. Zeresh found someone, a man who worked for a family that owned a herd of pigs, and he was willing to tell us about the happenings of the previous day.

The man spoke of one of the town's men who had been possessed by demons for years. He lived out at the burial caves and was a constant terror for the people who lived in the area. Even people passing through were subject to screaming by the man, some so much that they would not dare travel the road.

When Yeshua and His followers came to town, the demons inside the man started shouting, "Yeshua, Son of God Ha'Elyon (the Most High)! What do you want with me? I beg You, don't torture me."

For Yeshua had ordered the unclean spirit to come out of the man. Then, He asked the man, "What is your name?"

"Legion," he said because many demons had entered him. Instead of being tortured before their time, they asked to be sent to the pigs that were feeding on the hill.

Yeshua spoke one word, "Go."

The demons came out of the man and went directly into the herd of pigs, which ran, squealing, down the hill into the lake and drowned.

When the townspeople heard what had happened to the man and the herd of pigs, they asked Yeshua and His followers to leave their region.

Kalev asked if anyone knew where the group was headed, and one traveler from the south mentioned that he had seen a group of men coming from town and heading toward the direction from which he had come. We decided that had to be the group for which we searched.

Once again, we began walking, and I found out Kalev was right. The land in the area was not as hilly as the land on the other side of the lake. I thought that we had a really good time arriving in Beit-Anyah East of the Yarden (Bethany, East of the Jordan).

Still, by the time we arrived, it seemed that Yeshua and His followers had left a couple of days ahead of us. They were heading back to K'far-Nachum. They were following the Jordan River to the lake to catch a boat that was going north.

I felt like all the eyes of my companions were turned on me. The thoughts that I saw showing in those eyes were: "This was a wasted trip. We could have stayed on our side of the lake, in our own tents and beds, waiting for Him to return." Yet, I remember the discussion of the trip in an entirely different way. But I was not one to say, "I told you so."

I thanked the men for the information and turned toward the river to follow its banks until we got back to the Galil and the boat that we had left on the shore. It took over a week to get back to the boat and another two days to row across the lake and make our way to Moreda's house.

During our trip from the other side of the lake, we had a discussion about what to do this time. We had spent a great deal of time just trying to locate a man who was always on the move. It didn't seem like he spent too much time in one place at all. How would we be able to catch up with someone like that? We had all come to an agreement that it would be best for the group to return to camp and try to find a pattern in the movements of Yeshua.

I mentioned this in the presence of my mother, Moreda and Giesell. I know that they were disappointed in our decision but understood that it was something over which they had no control. They would continue to help us in any way that they could in order to find a solution to our problem. Mother mentioned that she would tell the other women that we were back and the daily provisions would begin the next day.

After eating a meal, we went back to camp and settled in for a long wait.

Following the trip that we had to endure and the letdown of not getting the healing that we were all looking forward to receiving, it was just nice to get back into camp, settle in our tents, and in our normal lives. We knew that whatever came, we would make it through together.

As time went on and the days all sort of ran together, I began to wonder if we had made the right choice. Even though I was still active in my morning routine of training, I did not have the strength to do as much running. I would mostly walk, sometimes fast, but other times, I would just shuffle along with no thought or direction in mind.

Most every day, when Mother, Giesell, or the other women from town would bring our daily provisions, they would bring news that had been brought in by travelers that had passed through the area. Many would tell of the great healings that were being done by Yeshua.

I was beginning to think that I had lost my chance, my only chance. If I could go back to the day when I first heard of the healing of the one who had the same disease that we in the camp did, I should have packed up my things and headed out. Traveling on my own, with that one goal in my mind, I know that I would have traveled faster. I would have been able to find the group that surrounded Yeshua, and I would have asked Him for healing for me and the rest of the men that were plagued by the same disease. After hearing so many stories of how He would show great compassion for those who were suffering, I know that He would not have denied that request.

I thought about my plan all day and well into the night. I rose the next day at first light and took out my old drawing sheets. I found my writing implements and began a note to David and Zeresh. I explained my desire to find Yeshua for healing and ask Him to return with me to the camp so that they all could receive it also. I asked them to pass the information on to the group along with Mother and Giesell, as I did not have a chance to write a separate note to them. They would have to hear about my decision second-hand, telling them to wait and that I would return. I would bring Yeshua so that all would be able to return to their families to spend the rest of their lives getting to know what it was like to belong to a family who would love them without being afraid of touching them or getting close to them.

I left the letter on my bed, took up a small traveling roll, and began my trip toward the lake. I knew that I would not have access to a boat this time, making plans as I walked along the shore toward the river where I could cross over to Beit-Tzaidah.

Not finding anyone in town who could help me, I continued on to the next town. As I walked a safe distance from the other travelers that seemed to be constantly walking the roads, I would hear that Yeshua and His group of "disciples" were seen going to Nazareth, which was where He lived His childhood. I knew that I was getting closer to finding the group.

I would pick up my speed as much as I could. I would eat a little bread while walking, not wanting to sit, believing if I did stop, I would be putting more distance between Yeshua and me. I had to find Him! I needed His help! But soon, I found out that even though my mind was telling me that I had to keep moving, my body just would not cooperate.

Eventually, I had to give in and rest. I found a small cave on the hillside, well away from the path traveled. I laid down and slept for a complete night and part of the next day. The sun was high in the sky when I finally awoke to find myself aching all over; I was hungry and reaching for my waterskin. I slowly drank all that I had. I knew that I would have to get down to the river so that I might refill my waterskin. With the thought in my mind that I had lost two days, I felt that I had let everyone down.

This began to frustrate me more than I ever imagined. Here I was, a strong man that was once a military man, but I was beginning to show the signs of not being the person Abba had always wanted me to become. I was looking more like a failure than I had ever thought possible. This was part of my training, the endless hours of moving over terrain, whether it be rocky or sandy, traveling along with small portions of rations that would have been something to which I would have been accustomed. I realized that my body had been going through a slight, but at the same time, an immense change because of the disease that continued to take over my skin and muscle tissue. I noticed, daily, the loss of little things, like the ability to hold a piece of fish tightly or to open my waterskin as easily as I did only days before. I wasn't sure how long I would be capable of doing the walking that I needed to do to find Yeshua and His disciples.

The random traveling continued for a few weeks, and I found myself thinking about Giesell more every day. The few times that I had seen her since she arrived in the area, she did seem like she had changed in her thinking of what would give her happiness in this life. It appeared that she was more concerned with others and what they were going through than she had in our past life together.

Maybe I was leaning toward giving our marriage another try, giving Giesell a second chance. But this would only be possible if I were to be healed. That's what I needed to accomplish first.

With that on my mind, I would head in the direction that I

had heard the group was spotted recently, yet arrived to find that they were no longer there. One day, I might hear stories of Yeshua in K'far-Nachum; the next, it was in Decapolis that someone had spotted Him. One group of travelers spoke of Him teaching throughout the country of Galilee. That was a big area of land that would have to be covered in order to find them. I was not sure where to start after hearing that news.

One particular day, I got to the point of just giving up. It was useless; I was hopeless. I would never be able to find my way to where Yeshua was so that I might ask Him for healing. Bitterness began to creep into my soul. Was this the way that things were going to end for me? Why was it that I could not find a way to catch up with Yeshua? I knew that I was able to accomplish many things, so why was I unable to do the simplest one of all?

A few minutes went by as I sat there, wallowing in my self-pity. Then, as when a flash of lightning lights up the sky during a storm, the words that I had spoken to David those months ago came into my mind, "You have to believe that there is a reason for all of this in your life. There has to be a reason for this disease that has taken over so much of our bodies. We have to be willing to wait and learn the reason."

I also remember the time that Giesell had first mentioned the change in her life since meeting Yeshua at the well. How she had been focused on herself and what she had wanted in her life. Now, she was thinking more of the people around her. She had been working with Mother so much since she had moved to K'far-Nachum. Moreda had told me many times about Giesell cleaning for Shabbat, and she was constantly cooking, not only getting meals ready for our camp but also for those who were living on the roads throughout the town and surrounding area. Mother had mentioned a few times that they never seem to run out of fish that they used for meals. The farmers around the town would send their sons with vegetables and grains that could be used for soups and breads. She would always thank Adonai for the provisions that they had to feed those who were in need. There were so many women willing to cook. Everyone seemed more focused on others around them since being visited by Yeshua.

Then, my thoughts went back to that time when I was out doing my daily training routine. That day when I had begun thinking that I should be able to catch up with Yeshua if I went out on my own. I had thought of asking for my healing and then the healing of the men at the camp. Yet, for some reason, I began to think that I was being selfish, thinking of myself first! What was that all about?

When we were younger, Mother had always taught us that we should always put others' needs above our own. We were not to consider ourselves better than anyone else. Adonai had created all the same. As I tried to remember the words, it was something like, "What we chose to do with what we have been given, that will bring from within us that which will make us stand out in our lives here."

No, let me try that again!

If we do not apply ourselves and the knowledge that we have, we could just go through life. But with the strength from within and the understanding of what is expected of us, not by man but by Adonai, that is what would bring us to excel in all things. I could become a physician or a teacher, or whatever I wanted to be; all it takes is using what is inside of me to excel in my life. While, at the same time, letting those around me know that they have the same opportunity that I have. The power that they need is inside of them. All that they need to do is listen to what is being said to them.

Those thoughts reminded me of that conversation that I had with Abba in regard to the trainees that had been placed under my command. He was saying the same thing but using the words which he knew best. Trainees might excel further than I did, but it was the training that I instilled in them that brought that "inner focus" that they needed to realize that they could go further. I was just the tool that was being used to get them to the point where they needed to be to reach out for something more, which brought me to the point where I thought that I had failed in being that same tool to be used by the men that surrounded me daily at the camp. Most of them were in worse shape than I was, and yet I was the one being selfish. They worked and existed as a group; when one was hurting, the others would come to his rescue and help him with anything and everything that was possible for them to do. Not one of them would have taken off on his own, trying to be "a hero" or showing that he was more capable of doing what needed to be done. That he alone could do what the others could not.

That night after the last piece of bread was eaten, I spent a few hours weeping. I didn't remember the last time that I just laid on the ground, crying like I did that night. I realized that I did not know where to turn, and there was no one there to let me know what I needed to do. Where was I to go? I felt as if I were all alone, and I did not have the strength to continue. I would just stay where I was and give up on this idea of ever being rid of the tzara'at.

Finally, weary from all the thoughts that had gone through my mind along with the ups and downs of emotions that I had experienced that day, I fell into a deep yet troubling sleep.

I had a dream, only it felt more real than most dreams that I had in my life. I was on the top of a hill, standing and looking out over the landscape that seemed to go on for miles. It reminded me of the solitary camp outside of Sh'khem after finding the first signs of the rash of being separated from my family. When I would walk and run up the mountain, I would look out over the land and see figures walking. Sometimes, they were in the distance; other times, just below where I was standing. Many times, there was a group of people traveling together. Occasionally, there might be a single individual walking alone or maybe pulling the reins of a donkey.

However, in my dream, there were no figures to be seen, no travelers, no donkey, only land. I was alone. Yet in my mind, in my soul, I felt that there was someone there with me. I turned and looked around but did not see anyone. I found a large rock and sat down to ponder what all of this might mean. Even though alone, as I looked out around the scene in front of me, I felt as if I were back at the beginning. The beginning of all of this turmoil that had been my life for what seemed to be a very long time. Was I supposed to focus on all the days that I had lived since this had begun? Or was there a particular time on which I needed to concentrate? Dreaming of this scene that looked so familiar brought up questions that I did not know how to answer.

All of a sudden, there stood a figure beside me, looking at me with a look of wisdom like I had never seen in a person. Maybe this was the one who could bring clarity to my thoughts. As I was forming questions in my mind about who he was and why he had come to me, thoughts came to me that gave me the answers before I could speak.

"Fear not! I am Gavri'el (Gabriel), and I have been sent to you by Adonai. He has seen the great struggle that is going on within you, and He understands that you feel like you are alone. It might seem to you at this point, but rest easy on the knowledge that you are not alone.

"Your mother, Maridi, speaks with Adonai without ceasing, asking for your safe return home. Your wife, Giesell, has begun to bring petitions to Adonai for the strength that you need to help you through your journey. Your sisters, Remah, Helgi, Moreda, and Delai, along with their husbands and children, also request that there would be people in your life that will help you in any way that they can so that you can return to your family. David and Zeresh have gotten the remainder of your companions to also speak on your behalf to Adonai, that the healing and the renewal of your spirit be completed even if the healing of your body has not taken place.

"Adonai has not completed His work in you and through you. He is continuing to do the work that is needed. You, in turn, will do the same for others that are in your life. There are still things that have been designed for you to achieve with the days that you have remaining on this earth. You will be given the strength that is necessary for you to fulfill what is needed. You will be able to achieve all things, and you will remember from whom you have received this power.

"Now, rest your body and mind, for the day will soon be dawning. After dawn, there will be no time for rest. You will begin to get ready for all that you must do for yourself, for your family, and for your friends." With those final words, he was gone, and I was again sitting on the rock. But I no longer felt like I was alone.

The next morning, refreshed and invigorated, I set out heading east toward the Galil, knowing that when I neared the water, I could turn toward the north, and it would lead me home.

While continuing on the journey, I did find that there were people willing to give me a portion of their food to sustain me. The thing that I found most puzzling was that some of them didn't really seem to want to help. It was something inside (or maybe outside) of them telling them to come close to this lonely figure that they saw while traveling the road and give him the provisions that would be needed for the day. I was grateful for that, knowing that I would not have to be hungry. I did not eat a lot at any time, just enough to keep my strength up in order to continue my journey. Yet, it seemed that whenever the food would run out, there would always be someone to come along to help me, supplying me with all that I needed. I began to believe that Adonai had not forsaken me, even after all that I had taken upon myself, trying to do things on my own. I seemed to have forgotten all that my mother had taught me while growing up. She would say,

"Adonai is always with us, even when we feel as if we are the only ones on earth. At times, we might feel like we are at the bottom and there is no possible way that we can get any lower. It might seem as if there is no one who is willing to help and no way of knowing how much more pain we have to endure. For us to be living the best life that we believe is our destiny, we have to remember that He will always be nearby. We only have to look up. And remember that things that we believe to be impossible can be accomplished when we bring our petitions to Adonai. That is exactly what He is waiting for us to do."

When I was growing up, it was hard for me to comprehend all that I was hearing. I mean, why would Adonai want to help me? I was just a boy; I was of no importance to anyone other than my parents. I was not as smart as some of the children from our neighborhood. I did not move as fast as the older boys, nor was I able to hold my own during the wrestling matches that we were coaxed to join.

So, why would someone as important as Adonai want to do anything for me?

Now, I am beginning to understand.

It was no longer imperative that I get to Yeshua or anyone else that had the healing powers that were required for the healing that I wanted to be done. I could still do great things while I am afflicted with tzara'at. It would not be around other people as the distancing issue still remained. But I could get back to camp and help my fellow sufferers. I could find ways to support them.

The important thing, I felt, was being open to what was critical in my own life. There was a part that I needed to play, and it was not traipsing all over the countryside on my own, on a quest of my own making. Whether the healing came or not, I realized that there was something that I had to do, as told by the messenger, Gavri'el. I was just hoping that I would be considered worthy of what it was that was being worked through me.

Yet, there was still this small voice that seemed to say that I was not good enough, not "in tune" with Adonai enough to be useful in anything. I tried my best not to listen.

That night, I rested, realizing in the morning, I would again begin my journey back to my family.

It took me longer than I want to say to make it back home. I went directly to Moreda's house. Mother was so glad to see me. She and Moreda began crying when they saw me standing in front of them. Needless to say, I became teary-eyed and overcome with emotion also. It seemed like a lifetime since we had been together.

Mother continued talking through it all. She spoke of how Delai and her husband, Yishai (Jesse), who actually preferred to be known as Jesse, had visited a couple of months ago. They had stayed for a few weeks before returning to Corinth. They were doing well and expecting their first child later in the spring. They had heard from Remah and Helgi. They and their families were also doing well. Remah now had three sons and two daughters. Helgi had one son and two daughters, with another child to be born in a few weeks.

I asked about Giesell, and Mother said that she was still in town, had made some friends, and was spending time between the two houses. She was expected to come back on the morrow, and

Mother was sure that she would be excited to see that I had returned safely to them.

Nothing was said about the message that I had David bring to them, the fact that I would return healed. I imagined that they could tell that I had failed in accomplishing that since I was still covered from head to foot and standing at a distance. I had been so positive that I would be able to achieve so much on my own and that this homecoming would be one worth remembering. But I was just so happy to be home that the words which were meant to come back to haunt me did not have any effect on me. I simply smiled and continued eating the soup and bread that Moreda had set before me while Mother continued telling me all that had occurred since I had been away.

A few minutes later, Moreda came out of the house with a bundle of cloth in her arms. I noticed a little movement and realized that she was holding a baby. She smiled at me and brought the baby as close as she could while being safe. Holding the bundle up so that I could see the face, she introduced me to her son, Micah. He was still tiny, I figured, not much more than a month old. I told Moreda that I was happy for her and Shim'on. She smiled her thanks and mentioned that he preferred to be known as Peter now. There was another thing that I was going to have to get used to, among all the other changes that I was sure that I would find out about once I got back to camp and into my regular routine.

Moreda asked me to stay for a day or two before heading back to the camp. She had some of Peter's old boating coverings that could be used to set up a tent in the yard for me to use for shelter. Mother would be pleased to have someone else to spend time with throughout the day. I was thankful to have the opportunity to spend time with family; therefore, I agreed to stay on for a few days but stated that the coverings were not necessary. I had gotten used to sleeping under the night sky.

Giesell sent word by a son of one of Mother's friends that she would be staying there for a few more days but that she would be returning to visit with them for Shabbat. Even though I was looking forward to seeing Giesell, I told Mother and Moreda that I needed to get to camp and let everyone know that I was back from my travels and doing well.

They agreed that I needed to get back to the group but would be very grateful if I would come back to visit every other week. Mother had mentioned that she was not making it out to the camp as much as she used to but had gotten a few younger women in the neighborhood to make the daily trip out there. The men were still getting all the care necessary.

After those days of bliss, having time with Mother, seeing Moreda taking care of her own family, and enjoying staying in one place for a while, I left to make the trip out to the camp and get back to the life that I had left behind.

I had not given up on the healing that was possible for me and the others that were afflicted as I was; it was only there were more important things in life to focus upon while waiting. I was extremely confident, within my soul, that the time for healing would come. I also knew that the waiting would be the hardest part!

As I walked down to the tents, the scene was just the way that I remembered it. A couple of tents were in worse shape than before; I guessed it was the weather that had taken its toll on the material. Maybe, we could find someone who could replace them.

Whenever there were footsteps heard on the rocks that lined the path toward the tents, there was always someone who would stick their head out to see who was approaching. This time was no different. I saw Asha peer around the tent flap and heard his voice calling out my name as he recognized me. Soon after that, more bodies were coming out of the tents to welcome me back.

Voices were flooding my ears, so many speaking at once that I couldn't understand what was being said, but I could tell that the greetings were genuine. A few minutes went by before everyone settled down. We all gathered benches and chairs together in order to sit and talk about things.

I quickly noticed that there were fewer men than when I had left. David spoke of Sha'ul and Akan dying just a few days after I had left on my journey, within days of each other. They fought the disease as long as they could, but in the end, they could not win.

I was saddened by the knowledge that despite all that I had attempted to do, going out on my own in order to find Yeshua and having Him return with me to camp so that these men would be able to get back to their families, that knowledge probably didn't bring comfort to either Akan or Sha'ul in their last hours.

And the little voice began: *Did I actually believe that I could have accomplished such a feat? What made me think that I was so invincible and so much better than anyone else that I was positive I would bring healing to those around me by finding Yeshua and somehow talking Him into making the trip back here? What a failure I turned out to be!*

I began to ponder those things as the conversations continued around me. After moments of going back over things that I had faced over the last few months, I came to the realization that what had transpired over that time was what needed to happen to get me to the place where I was to be—here in this time, in this place, with these men. I could have stayed with the group from the very beginning and journeyed through the same days and nights through which they had come.

Remembering my mindset from the time that we, as a group, had returned to camp to the time that I had left on my solitary trip, I believe that I would have become wearier about the life that we were forced to live. I needed that time by myself in order to find myself. I had become so desperate with the desire to be cured. Even though I thought by including others in need of healing, I was somehow not being selfish and thinking only about what I wanted, what I needed.

Case in point, sitting there with all the men talking to me as though I was actually listening to what was being said. Instead, I was focused on things in my mind and in my life, being selfish. When was I going to learn that there were other people in the world, even in this camp, who were hurting and just wanted someone to listen to them? Was I so far into myself that I could not see the people around me and understand that they might be having the same fears, the same insecurities that I am having?

I stood up to stretch my legs, which felt numb at that moment. Returning to my chair, I focused more on what was being said by my companions, trying to learn how things were affecting them. Those seven men had been confidants for years before David, Zeresh, and I had joined them in the camp. The loss of their two friends would bring about unspeakable pain; they would need someone to listen and understand what they were feeling.

Soon, I was experiencing the sense of routine that I was familiar with, as food was brought in by the women of the town. We ate and talked throughout the remainder of the daylight hours. Samuel, along with his friend, Keylie, brought the water vessel from the well. Both of them welcomed me back, saying that I had been greatly missed by everyone.

As we began our ritual of resting, Zeresh had everyone stop in order for him to say words of thanksgiving to Adonai for my safe return. When that was completed, we all slept, knowing that we were together once more.

The next morning, I was surprised to come back from my morning run, I mean, walk, to find Mother and Giesell coming down from town. They had brought the morning meal for us, but I could tell that was not the only reason that the two of them had made the trip. They set the provisions down in the usual spot and motioned for me to come apart from the others for a private conversation.

Giesell was distraught. Mother explained that she had received word from Sh'khem that her mother was very ill. Giesell wanted to return but did not know of anyone who was traveling in that direction. They were wondering if I would be willing to go with her to see her safely to her mother's home.

I, of course, said yes. Plans were made for Giesell to gather a few of her belongings and return the next morning early to begin the journey.

After they had left for town, I spoke to David and Kalev about accompanying Giesell and me to Sh'khem. They agreed to go, and we mentioned this to the rest of our group in order to prepare them for our departure the next day.

The three of us began our rest a little earlier than usual, knowing the roughness of the countryside in which we would be heading; we would need all the strength that we could find to make it to our destination.

Not surprisingly, Zeresh arose when we did. When Giesell arrived, and we were setting off on our journey, he spoke to Adonai, asking for a protective shield to be around us, an attentive eye to be ever watching over us as we traveled the roads, for healing to begin on the mother of Giesell and the safe return to everyone to their family.

As we left camp, heading south, I thought to myself that we

might have asked Zeresh to come with us. After all, he did have family in town. Even though they were Rivkah's parents, I am sure that they still considered Zeresh part of their family. But with his condition worse than ours, I wasn't sure that he would have agreed to make the journey; he would have said that he would only slow us down, and Giesell needed us to get her to her mother as soon as we could. He was like that, always thinking of others more than himself.

Ever since his confession, so long ago, about him being the reason that I had become afflicted, he had become more focused on his faith in Adonai. I am sorry to say that he was more in tune with his beliefs than I had been over the past few years. I said my own prayer to Adonai and asked Him to bring about the change needed in me so that I might be more like Zeresh.

Traveling that day was rough at times. David took the lead for a while, Giesell walking behind him with Kalev and I walking behind her. We rested and ate when we needed, switching the walking procession around with Kalev leading for a while; then, it was my turn to lead. When the sun began to descend behind the mountains, we would stop for the night and awaken the next morning to begin again.

On the eighth day, we entered the main part of Sh'khem. David and I both remarked that there was very little that had remained the same as we remembered. Giesell said that after the visit from Yeshua, things had changed a great deal throughout the town, especially in the lives of many of the people who were living there. People just seemed to like each other more; they were willing to help those who were less fortunate, and things that were done in the past were not brought up again. And she knew that it had to be the result of the teachings that they had heard while Yeshua was in town. There could not be any other explanation for the transformation that had taken place in so many lives.

We walked Giesell to her mother's house and mentioned that we would stay if she wanted us to do so. Otherwise, we would probably go out to see where our old camp had been set up. She had mentioned, on the trip down, that the buildings that were promised to be built were there, but at the time that she had left, there was no one living in them.

At this time, she asked that we stay for a few minutes until she found out how her mother was doing and would bring word to us that we might not worry throughout the night. Across from the house was an empty field in which we could wait so as not to be in the way of anyone coming to or from the house.

As we waited, I motioned around the area, explaining to Kalev of the surrounding houses and buildings. David remembered a few things that I had forgotten, and the time that we waited for Giesell seemed to fly by. Soon, I noticed that she had come out of the house and was walking toward us. I could tell the news that she had received while inside was not good news at all.

Wishing that I could comfort her, I steeled myself against moving toward her and waited with the others for her to come over to us. She said that her mother was gravely ill, and the physician that had come out did not believe that she would last through the week. We all tried to speak words of comfort to her, along with words of sympathy. Much beyond that, there was nothing that we could do.

Giesell thanked us for accompanying her on the journey home and said that if we wanted to get back to K'far-Nachum, she understood. Looking at the other two, I felt their agreement as I said that we would be staying in the area for a while to see if her mother did get better; that Adonai was still able to bring healing to those who needed it. Giesell then spoke the words that I and maybe both David and Kalev were thinking.

"It would be nice if Yeshua would stop by Sh'khem for another visit." There was wonder in her voice and a thoughtful look in her eyes, letting us know that she believed that if Yeshua were in town, He could heal her mother as He had healed my mother when she had the fever.

"Giesell, that is possible; you never know," Kalev spoke to her as she turned toward the house.

She smiled a weak smile and said that she would see us soon. We spoke our goodbyes and headed up the lane toward the outskirts of town.

As we walked, we noticed that some things remained the same. There was the old military training field, and the tents could be seen in the distance. It took us a while to get out of town and to the spot on the hill that had been my shortcut from town to camp. The brush was a bit overgrown, showing me that it had been some time since anyone had walked that path, at least on a regular basis. David and Kalev followed me since I was the one who remembered every twist and turn that we needed to take to get back to the camp.

When we arrived, we were surprised to see a couple of figures sitting on a bench outside one of the hovels that had been erected for shelter for those who were in need of them. The two looked up as we approached and were shocked to see us coming so close to them.

David held up his hand in greetings to them and spoke, telling them that we were visitors from up north who had lived in the area a few months in the past. He introduced us, and we found that their names were Manulle and Lazerith. They were from Raphana, which was one of the Decapolis cities on the east side of the Jordan. They had heard of this place being built for those afflicted with tzara'at and had traveled to see it. When they found out that no one was living here, and since they did not have any close family, they decided to make it their home.

We sat and talked for the greater part of the evening, getting to know each other. Finally, after the weariness of the day overtook us, we spoke of getting sleep, and they showed us the areas that were not occupied. We gathered our bundles and went to rest.

Early the next morning, we awoke to hear a familiar voice. We came out to see Dorlas had brought the day's provisions and was also bringing the news of the town. She squealed with delight when she noticed David and me. In fact, she looked as if she were going to come over and give hugs to both of us, then stopped herself, which made us all break into laughter. We introduced Kalev and sat down to enjoy our meal and the conversation with Dorlas. I had forgotten how long she could go on about things that were of so little importance. But she felt it was her responsibility to keep us apprised of everything that occurred throughout the countryside. She did bring news that Giesell's mother was still with us, and the physician was doing all that he could to help during this time.

After hours of listening to the happenings in the lives of people in town, we rose to our feet, groaning from the stiffness that was felt after sitting for such a long time. But we enjoyed visiting with Dorlas, and she, in turn, told us that she was glad that we were back in the area.

When she had left, each of us was busy with our own thoughts. Manulle took the eating utensils to be cleaned while Lazerith straightened things on the table.

David, Kalev, and I discussed whether or not to go into town to see how Giesell was holding up and find out how her mother was doing, but we decided to wait a few days. We did not want to add to the distress that the family would be going through at a time such as this.

Early on the third morning, David and I took off for town. Kalev decided that he would remain with Manulle and Lazerith. As we gathered our coverings, David stated that it would probably be for the best. Kalev had been having more difficulty holding a spoon in order to feed himself, and many times, he would ask one of us to hold a cup to his lips so that he might have a drink of water. We realized that the disease had begun to take more of his strength away than he was willing to admit, and we wondered how much more time he had left with us.

As we walked the path to the house, I saw Giesell coming through the doorway as if she had known that we would be arriving at that time. When we came closer, I noticed that she had been crying. Before we could get any greetings out, she told us that her mother had died during the night. She had been in so much pain; everyone was relieved that she didn't have to endure it any longer.

The body was to be buried next to her father the following day, and as far as the rituals that they would be observing, I was not sure since the family did not practice the Jewish faith. We delivered our sympathy to Giesell and asked that she pass them on to her family also.

She didn't have too much to say, and we didn't want to take up the time that she needed for other things. I know that she would have to prepare herself for those who would be arriving to pay their respects. I told her that I would check back in a few days to see how she was doing and what plans she might have for the future. She gave a small smile and returned to the house. David and I turned to walk back to camp.

The next few days went by slowly and uneventfully. There were the typical daily chores and the conversations with Dorlas, but other than that, nothing worth mentioning.

On the sixth day, I decided that I had waited a reasonable amount of time and gathered my things, so I took off for town. This time, David suggested that he remain at the camp so that he could help Kalev with his day. We had been taking turns with our friend's care, but David knew that I wanted to make this trip to speak to Giesell.

I arrived at midday, moving over to stand in the field so that I could be seen from the house.

As I waited there, I thought about Giesell and the relationship that she had with her family. During the span of time that we were together, we would visit from time to time. As far as I noticed, they were not really close to each other. Maybe that has changed as time went by, but I am not sure. I was unable to imagine what she was planning on doing at this period of her life.

While I stood there, looking to see if I could see her figure through the doorway, my attention was caught by a small tree that sprang from the ground at such an angle that I stood in amazement that it even survived. About two feet off the ground, it splintered from the main truck, or what would be considered a trunk, beginning to grow in an entirely different direction.

Along the branch were smaller growths that seemed to come out from the bark but did not grow anymore. As my eyes continued to follow the branch, I noticed a big curve as if something had been placed in that area where the tree was growing, and it caused the growth of the branch to twist and turn. It had to adapt in order to continue its journey. There were still more little "stubs" that came out of the branch, some growing more than others, still part of that main branch. After more growth, the branch seemed to flourish and gather strength. Finally, it began to look like a healthy tree that saw new growth with many branches off-shooting their way toward the sky.

At a certain point up the branch, I noticed one branch that seemed to have grown on its own. It was as if that smaller branch, with its own strength, was trying to fuse with the other one. I returned my gaze to the smaller branch, following it back down to where I could see it connected with that original branch before the curving had begun.

I had never before, or any time since, seen a tree that was so oddly shaped and was of itself, I believe, a wonder—even a curiosity. How anything that had begun with such a small growth out of the ground could then become such a tree; well, let's just say that it really messed with my mind. Yet then, the wonders of nature, I was never one who said I understood those.

Noticing movement much further out from where I was looking at the time, I saw that Giesell was coming out of the house. She came across to me, and we talked for a while. She said that all her brothers were taking care of the family things, getting everything settled about the house and the land.

Caleb, who, along with his family, had been living with her mother since their father had died, would be staying there. Neer and Joram lived close by and would be helping in any way that was needed. Giesell wasn't sure what she would be doing, but for the foreseeable future, she would be staying with Caleb. Maybe in the next year or two, she would find out what she needed to do with the rest of her life. At this time, she was unsure.

I told her that I understood and wanted to help however I could. She mentioned if I asked Moreda to pack up the things that she had left, maybe there would be travelers coming back this way who might agree to bring them to her. I told her that as soon as I returned to K'far-Nachum, I would have Moreda take care of her things.

As I turned to go, I let her know that if she needed anything, all she had to do was get a message to me, and I would be there as soon as I could make the trip. I would also keep sending her word to let her know how things were going with me. Truthfully, I didn't know if I would ever see her again; there were too many things that had come between us. I wasn't sure whether we could ever have anything like we had in the past.

I walked back to camp, thinking about the feelings that I had for Giesell. Yes, I did still love her as I did when we were first married. There was nothing that I wouldn't do for her. Even with all the things that she had done after I had become afflicted with this disease, I still felt that same anticipation and excitement every time I was close to her. I wanted to hug her, comfort her and let her know that I would take care of her for the rest of my life.

This did bring about a bit of surprise within me as I remembered the reaction that I had after the long conversation that occurred when Giesell had first arrived at the camp on the outskirts of K'far-Nachum. But one thing that I remember my parents always agreeing on, in all my time growing up, was that everyone deserves a second chance. And during my traveling days earlier that year, I realized that it was true! We should not judge people on one incident; they might have been having a bad day and said something that they should not have said. Or maybe there was something that was done to them, and the way that they reacted was unexpected. No one is perfect, and *we* should be the ones that know most of all. Everyone does deserve another opportunity to make right the things that they have done wrong. At the very least, we could give them the chance to tell their side of the story.

Suddenly, I stopped in my tracks as a random thought came into my mind, *What if the situation was only one person's perspective?*

I looked around for a place off of the path where I might be able to sit and think this thing through until I understood what I was thinking. I found such a place and sat on the ground, staring out at the horizon.

What came to my mind was an incident from my childhood when my friends Yosef and Ammi were still in my life. There were a few days that were now flashing through my thoughts as I sat, trying to remember the details.

I was going to meet with Ammi, and together, we were going over to join in some games with Yosef and a few of his relatives that were visiting from the south.

When we came together on the side of the road, Ammi was excited about something and could not wait to tell me about it.

"Gaius, you will not believe the good fortune that I have received this day! I was walking along the road on my way to meet you and saw something glittering in the sunlight. I ran over to see what was lying in the dirt, and this is what I found." He reached out his hand and, unclenching it, showed me a coin. "It's a denarius, and it is worth quite a lot, don't you think?"

I was not sure, as I had never seen a denarius before that day. He let me hold it, and I looked at it closely. Ammi was so happy to have found such a treasure and began speaking about what he could buy with such a coin. I mentioned to him that Yosef was waiting for us to arrive at the house. Ammi spoke of needing to take care of the treasure that he had found and that he would meet me at Yosef's house.

While I continued the walk up the road, Ammi ran back to his house to put the coin somewhere safe. He never did make it to Yosef's house that day.

A couple of days later, when all three of us were together, Ammi mentioned when he had spoken to his parents about his plans for the denarius. They were going to make a trip to Shomron, where there were more merchants selling goods around the town. He would be able to pick out whatever he wanted to buy.

The next day, with Ammi out of town, it was just Yosef and me. He had made the trip to my house, and as soon as I saw him coming down the lane, I could tell something was wrong. I asked him about it when he came into the yard.

He started speaking about looking for a coin that his uncle had given him when they had stopped by on their trip to Nain. Yosef had put it in a place that he knew would be a great hiding place, but when he had gone to get it that morning, it was gone. Then, he started accusing Ammi of taking the coin a few days before when he had come over to the house. Yosef had shown him the coin, and they were both in awe of what could be purchased with it.

For a long while, he talked of Ammi taking the coin and then making up the story of finding it on the road.

I was shocked to think that one of my friends would take something from another one of his friends. I really didn't want to believe that Ammi did take the coin from Yosef, but I did not see Ammi when he claimed that he found it on the road. All I knew was what I had been told. I had no reason to say that is not exactly the way that it happened. There was no previous time throughout all the years that we had known each other where we were not totally honest with each other. But still, all the things that Yosef was saying began to stick in my mind as being facts. And with Ammi not being there to tell me any different, I started to believe it.

Things were never really the same between us after that incident, and it was only about a month later when Yosef and his family moved out of town. And Ammi was no longer allowed to associate with me.

As I thought about it while I sat in the field, I came to think that if I had been given the chance to speak to Ammi after that time, I would have known that he had found the coin on the road just as he said. Yosef must have been wrong in accusing Ammi of taking his coin. Maybe, he himself had moved it and had forgotten where he had placed it. I realized that it could be as simple as that!

A second chance would have been all that was needed to keep a friendship intact. Who knows how our relationship would have turned out if only there had been an opportunity to make things right?

Now, it was time for me to give that to Giesell. I wanted to make up for the lost time that had taken up so much of our lives that should have been lived together. I wanted to make her happy, to see her smile again. I just wish that I could do that.

Upon my return to camp, I sat with the others and told them of the happenings of the day. Now that things were settled, maybe it was time for David, Kalev, and me to return to our camp. Manulle and Lazerith looked saddened at the prospect of being just the two of them again. David told them that they would be welcome to come back with us, mentioning that we did not have the space that they had, but the people of the town were very generous with their help to all of us. We would probably stay a few more days before heading back. There was time for them to discuss it between the two of them and let us know their decision.

Four days later, there were five of us making the trip back north. I had made another trip into town to talk to Giesell, letting her know that we were going back up to K'far-Nachum. She wished us a safe journey, and that was all that was said between us.

We also informed Dorlas of our upcoming journey. We thanked

her for all the services that she had given to all of us over the past years. We asked that she let all those who had been generous in their giving of provisions, time, and labor in all that they had done for the inhabitants of the camp know that our thankfulness was unending. We would ask Adonai to give special blessings to all.

While we were traveling, David spoke of the men that we were returning to and how we had become a family and took care of each other. He told them about my mother and the other women that would prepare food for us, the young men that would bring us water, and about life in general in K'far-Nachum.

We had to take our time and rest as Kalev was still having issues with his strength. When we were able, David and I would carry him, our arms around his waist and his arms around our necks. Other times, when the path was narrow, we would take turns carrying Kalev on our backs. He didn't weigh too much, and we were surprised each morning when we found that our friend had made it through another night. Yet, when we awakened and moved over to where he slept, we spoke a sincere "Thank You" to Adonai for allowing us another day together.

It was the end of the third week when we rounded the bend, heading on the last part of our journey into camp. We were all weary from traveling and wanted to rest for a very long time.

After being welcomed back and eating our meal together, David and I spoke of what had happened with Giesell and her family. Everyone seemed to agree that it was the right thing for her to do—staying with her family. They would need time to grieve their loss together.

Thinking about family, I wanted so much to take the walk to town to see Mother and Moreda. But the thought of getting back on my feet and walking more steps was not anything I wanted to think about at that time. I remained there, sitting with the men and engaging with them in conversation.

Hevel and Kalev dozed off while we were sitting while Elah and Zeresh took Manulle and Lazerith to show them where they could unpack their belongings. We all went to sleep early that night, knowing that rest would be the best thing for us.

Early the next morning, I rose and gathered my clothing. I was preparing to make the trip into town. I knew that if I waited until the others awoke, they would want to travel with me. With Kalev being in a worse condition than just a few weeks ago and David spending so much time caring for him while we were away, I thought it best that they just stay in one place for a time. Most of all, it had been a while since it was just me that showed up at Moreda's home for a visit. I left a note beside Zeresh's bed and went toward town.

People were just beginning to stir by the time I made it to the edge of town. I kept my distance as was my normal practice and made it quickly to the lane leading to the house. I could see my mother through the open doorway, preparing the morning meal. I began to wonder if she still missed Abba. I guess it was the feelings that I had for Giesell and knowing that she was further away now. Perhaps, it was just me trying to believe that we would see each other again and yet having that feeling of loneliness inside of me. I shook my head slightly to clear those thoughts and put my mind on things there at that moment. When I had gotten closer, I called out to my mother and noticed her stop her activities and turn in my direction.

I saw a smile come to her face and heard her call to Moreda that I had arrived home at last. That brought a smile to my face, thinking that she would have considered this as my arrival home. To think that was possible—having time back with my family, to sit close to them and talk, to greet them with hugs and kisses, what

I wouldn't give if only I could do just that!

The two of them came out the door with joyful sounds of greetings. I noticed that they looked well as they entered the yard and motioned for me to sit down. I turned, and there was my chair, right where it had been when I left. I sat down, and Moreda brought out water to fill the cup that still remained on the table while Mother brought out plates of food for all of us to enjoy the meal together.

They asked questions about the trip and the outcome of Giesell's visit. They were saddened by the news of her mother's death but were glad that she was able to spend those last days with her. I believe that they expected to see Giesell with me, so I told them of the happenings in Sh'khem and of the decision that Giesell had made to remain with her family at this time. I think that they could tell that I was not convinced that was the best thing for either of us. I told them that it was her decision and I was not in any position to tell her otherwise.

They asked about David and Kalev after saying that they had been out to the camp at least twice a week in the schedule that they had arranged with other women throughout the neighborhoods. They made mention that they had even gotten a few of the husbands who were willing to help bring in water so that responsibility did not always fall upon the older boys of the families that were helping. I asked how they had been able to do that when no one had been able to accomplish that in the past.

Moreda mentioned that Peter, Yeshua, and the men traveling with them had made a stop in the town a few weeks before. Yeshua spoke to all who would listen on how we should help others that were unable to help themselves. They told of many that were healed, the great teaching that was being spoken in towns and villages. He had actually been heard speaking against the synagogue leaders.

Then, Moreda spoke of the sayings that Peter had told her, "Yeshua said the Torah teachers and the P'rushim (Pharisees) are hard-hearted, closed-minded, and interested only in trapping Him. That is why they are constantly looking for something that they might bring before the people to show that Yeshua is not the Mashiach that we have been told is coming. But Peter believes that *Yeshua is the One* who had been promised to us."

She went on talking for a very long time, talking about things that were spoken on so many topics and the parables that were being told to the multitudes.

Peter had spoken of the parables of which Yeshua spoke to them, some to the crowds, yet other parables only when the twelve were alone with Him.

There was one parable about a farmer sowing seeds, of which some fell along the path, and the birds came and ate the seed. Other seeds fell on the rock, and they came up, but the plants withered because there was no water. Some seeds fell among the thorns, which choked the plants as they tried to grow. Still, other seeds fell on good ground and were able to produce enough grain to feed many people.

When asked about the meaning of the parable, Yeshua explained that the seed was the word of God. Many people, upon hearing the word, were along the path, and the devil would take the word away from their hearts so they would not believe it. Other hearers of the word would have joy when they heard it, but the word would not take root so that it would grow. The words spoken to those who were among the thorns would let the pressures of the world, along with the worries, the riches, and the pleasures, choke out the word, and they would remain immature.

Only the word that fell on the ears of those with a good heart, who hear the word, keep the word, and preserve it through all of life's mishaps, would show the word through themselves. Others would believe because of that word flowing out of those who believe.

Peter kept up the conversation about the parables that continued over a range of subjects; there was one about the net, the pearl of great price, the lost sheep, and a lost coin.

One evening after dinner with Yeshua and the rest of the disciples, Peter stayed at the house as the others departed for the night. They would all be leaving to go to Ephraim in the morning. While sitting around the table before clearing the dishes away, Peter had wanted to tell them about one more parable of which Yeshua had spoken. It was a parable of a good Samaritan.

Moreda paused at that point in her telling of the story to take a drink of water. Mother looked over at me and smiled. I returned the smile, thinking that Mother was agreeing with me that the length of any conversation with Moreda could go on for hours. I often wondered, *If she ever got a sore throat and actually had to be quiet and still for one whole day, would she be able to endure it?*

A minute later, she continued with her story. Yeshua spoke of a traveler who was leaving Yerushalayim heading down to Yericho when he was attacked by robbers and left for dead on the side of the road.

I sat there looking first at Moreda and then at Mother as Moreda shared with me the story that she had heard from Peter. The man, as he was lying on the side of the road, called for help but was unable to get help from a cohen or a Levi. He was finally treated by a man who bandaged up his wounds, put him on a donkey, and took him to an inn. He stayed with the wounded man, caring for him, and made arrangements for the innkeeper to watch over the man as he healed from the beating that he had experienced.

I know that the shock that I felt was beginning to register on my face because the smile on my mother's face grew as she watched my reaction to the words spoken.

Finally, when Moreda completed her telling of the parable, I made a motion with my hand toward Mother and asked her, "How did He know?"

She then spoke quietly, "Adonai knows everything. Yeshua is the Son of Adonai; therefore, He knows all things as well. He may not have been anywhere that you could have seen Him, but Adonai is ever present with all of us. Just as we are given words of wisdom to speak to our children or to others that are needing comfort or encouragement, I am sure that Yeshua is given words of encouragement from His Father, which He passes on to strengthen many that are in need of them. Maybe that is how He would have known about the good deed that you had done. He would tell that story to show others that they can help out their neighbors, even if they don't know that person."

Moreda looked questioningly at both of us, and Mother just made the statement that she would explain it to her a little later.

That was all that Moreda needed to begin speaking again, but this time, she was telling other stories that had been told to them by other people besides Peter and the disciples.

There were groups of people coming from all directions who had heard of the teachings of Yeshua; others had said that they had been in the groups who heard the Rabbi telling His parables. Many of them did not understand what point He had been trying to make, but as He was willing to take on the Pharisees, He *had* to be the One who would lead the rebellion against the Roman Empire, and we would be able to regain our lands for our people.

After hearing that, I was concerned about what Peter had gotten himself into—this following of a man where there were so many different things being said. Which was the right one? What were people to believe? Was he indeed the Mashiach, or was he another one of those zealots that you heard who was trying to make trouble in order to lead another uprising against the rulers of the country? How could I know what decision I was going to have to make in order for the word to begin growing in me?

Moreda had to go into the house as she heard the voice of her child crying out for her attention.

Mother saw the confusion in my eyes and, with her voice, just as she has always done, comforted me with words that only a mother could get you to believe.

"Gaius, you know what is in your heart and what it is trying to tell you. Don't let other people tell you what you believe. That is up to you. Adonai will lead you in the direction that you are supposed to travel." She rose from where she had been sitting and began gathering up the dishes and cups to take them into the house for cleaning. Before she left, other words were spoken, "All I know is that whenever Yeshua is present in this house, I am more aware that the presence of Adonai is also with us." As she walked through the door, I took my eating utensils over to a small bucket of water sitting at the side of the house and cleaned them, placing them back on the table when I was finished.

While I was doing that, I pondered on these words that Mother had spoken. I wanted to believe, truly I did. Yet, there was that slight whisper of a voice that kept repeating, *What if you are wrong?* For that question, I had no answer.

I stayed a few days with Mother and Moreda. I saw that Micah had become a chubby little boy and that Moreda, at times, had to use all her strength in order to hold him still. Mother said that once he learned to walk, he would be able to rid himself of all that "baby fat." She said that it had been the same for me, but since I could not remember that time in my life, I had to take her word for it. There was no one around that could tell me any different.

At the end of the fourth day, I made mention that I needed to return to camp and see how the others were faring. I told them both that I would be starting out early in the morning, so we said our goodbyes that evening. I had been resting well since I had come home and knew whatever awaited me back at camp, I would be able to handle it.

By the time I arrived at camp, the men had begun stirring and gathering together what bread had been left over from the night before. We always would keep a little bread overnight because we knew that it was too early to expect provisions of the day. All of the women that were helping us had families of their own and would be taking care of them first, as it should be. Then, the food was cooked and gathered to be delivered to the camp. The water was brought later in the day, and we always had plenty to go around until the next visitation.

We spent our day going through our routine. We had done this for so long that it was part of our nature to go from doing one thing to the next until we had completed the morning's chores. When we had completed that, the food would have arrived, and we would sit down for our midday eating.

Zeresh, as his daily habit, said the b'rakhah, asking for Adonai to be with us all, to give Kalev the strength that he needed to make it through another day, and thanking Him that there were such people in the world that would give of their food and their time in order to care for those who could not care for themselves.

This day, instead of closing his prayer at this time, he continued to speak, "We know that there have been things learned these past few days that have us confused. We also know that You are the One who is able to help us realize what is right and what needs to be done. I ask that You would open our spirits up to know when we are to be ready to do what You would have us do. Give us wisdom to know what we should do on this day."

When he had finished speaking, I sat there for a few minutes, looking down at the plate that was placed before me. What had just happened? Why would Zeresh say such words in a prayer when he had never done that at any time previous?

When I raised my eyes from my plate, I saw that Zeresh was looking straight at me as if I were the only one at the table. I felt my face becoming flushed. I could not understand why. I had no reason to be disturbed by anything that had been said, yet I believe that I felt as if Zeresh could see what was in my mind and in my heart.

Somehow, we made it through the meal without any questions that were too pressing. Of course, the men wanted to know how my family was doing, and I answered all of their inquiries to their satisfaction.

After the completion of the meal, we all went back to our routines, and I was able to stay away from Zeresh and his prying eyes. I had to sort out my thoughts and find out not only what was bothering me so much with the words that he had spoken but also the look that had passed between us. I took my time doing my routine of training for the day, and it was well past our next meal time when I completed them. I walked from the camp some distance away and sat down on the ground next to a boulder on which I promptly leaned back, deep in thought.

As I sat, I began to remember the dreams that I had months before as I had been on the journey to find Yeshua and His followers. I remember seeing Gavri'el, the messenger from Adonai, and the instructions that he had brought to me. I still had things that I was meant to accomplish while I was here. Since receiving that directive, have I done anything? What have I achieved over the past few months? I couldn't think of a single thing.

Sure, I had made trips from K'far-Nachum to Sh'khem, to both camps at which I had lived. Now, I was back just sitting on the ground, focusing on myself instead of thinking about others.

I began feeling certain thoughts come flooding into my mind. What would I be able to do for others? I couldn't even get close to people without them backing away from me after the word "unclean" came across my lips. If I touched anything, no one would pick it up because it was considered unclean. There was nothing I could do, so how in the world would Adonai say that I had a mission to begin? I suddenly dropped my chin to my chest and sobbed quietly. Then, I heard a voice calling my name. I did not recognize the voice. Again, I heard,

"Gaius, are you ready?"

I stood to my feet, turning in a complete circle, yet seeing no one.

Once more, the voice spoke, "Be ready."

I stood quietly, leaning against the rock by which I had just been sitting, and waited for a few minutes. There were no more words to be heard. I looked skyward and thought I saw a glimpse of a familiar face, but in an instant, it was gone!

I began to wonder if I was going mad. Hearing voices? Right! Seeing a face in the clouds? Ha! There was no way that I was going to tell anyone about these past few minutes. People would believe that I was touched or possessed by a demon! I was beginning to think that myself.

As I turned to head back to camp, I saw Hevel heading toward me. He was actually running. I could not remember the last time that I saw Hevel moving so quickly. It must be something really urgent that would bring him out to look for me. I began to worry. It might be that Kalev had taken a turn for the worse, maybe even dying. And here I was, out on my own, focused on myself again. Was I ever going to learn?

I walked down the path to meet him, calling out for him to stop and wait where he was; I would come to him. I knew that if he continued to run toward me, he would be so out of breath that I would not be able to understand his words. While he was standing waiting for me to come to him, at least he would have a few minutes to catch his breath. Then, he could relay the message that he had been sent down to deliver. Even strolling down as slowly as I did, he was still breathing hard when I arrived by his side. For a few minutes, we both leaned against rocks while waiting for Hevel to be able to speak.

"Gaius, your sister has just arrived at the camp. She has something of great importance to tell you. Asha did not believe that he could find you, so Zeresh sent me. David was sent out to look for you by the sea. I think that we should hurry back to camp as she seemed to be in quite a haste to speak to you."

I agreed. As we began the walk toward camp, I began to think about what could have brought Moreda out of town at this time of day. I thought of Mother. Maybe something had happened to her this morning after I had left. I began to hurry my pace in order to get to my sister. It only took a few minutes until I could see Moreda standing in front of the tents waiting for me. The others were sitting at the table, which still held their meal.

Hevel went over to the table as I walked toward Moreda. I saw David returning from the other direction. He waved as he saw that

I had been brought back to camp.

As I stopped before her, I asked if something had happened to our mother, and she said no, it was nothing like that. Mother was doing well and was at the house looking after Micah. She had been sent to bring the message because she could walk faster than Mother. I waited for her to speak. Instead, she looked around and asked if there was a place where she could sit down. It was true that she could walk faster than Mother, but that did not mean that the walk had not made her tired and in need of rest. I motioned to the other side of the table where we had placed chairs for such a time as this. When we had visitors from town come out who wanted to stay and visit, to ask how everyone was doing and what was needed to help make it through our days.

Moreda sat down, and I saw her slip off her shoes. She had always been one who liked to go barefoot whenever possible. I smiled a little at that endearing little habit of hers that I remembered from our childhood. She arranged her dress so that it was not noticeable to anyone else. Then, she spoke,

"Gaius, we received a message today from Peter. He said that Yeshua and the group were leaving Dalmanutha heading for Yerushalayim."

Yerushalayim! Did Moreda not realize how many miles we would have to travel to make it to Yerushalayim? Was she aware of how long of a trip like that would take ten men who were all in some sort of decay from this disease that we had raging through our bodies?

She continued, "They have a few towns that they are going to stop in on the way. I talked it over with Mother, and we came up with the idea that if you and your friends were to leave and start the trip to the border between Galil and Shomron, there would be a greater chance that you would find them. We know that they will have to pass by the area sooner or later. If you are in the area, I am sure that someone traveling the roads would be able to tell you when a group was noticed coming your way. Peter says that they have quite a large group that follows them now. Yeshua could heal you all. I know that He can."

She leaned forward just a little and reached out as if to take my hand in hers. "Please, Gaius, do it for Mother and me. Mother needs to have you back in her life. She is not getting any younger. There are many days I do not want her walking out here to deliver food to you, even though I know it is a good thing that the other families and we are doing. And you know how she is; there is no way that I or anyone else will stop her from doing things that she knows she is capable of doing. Whether it is for your group or any other person who comes her way, she will continue to help them. I am just afraid that if she goes on this way, making all these trips, one day she will not be able to make it back home."

She wiped tears from her eyes and steadied her voice before she spoke, "I need to have my only brother back in my life. Even though, when we were growing up, I considered you a pain because it fell upon me as the sister just older than you to take care of you even more than Remah or Helgi. They were older and had to focus more on things that would make them a good wife and a good mother. I still loved you and wanted you to have a great life, no matter what you decided to do with it. I know that Abba would have been proud of you. Whether or not you had followed in his footsteps going into the military or striking out on your own as you wanted to do. If you had followed your dream about the designing of buildings, yes, Abba would have put up a fuss for months. But eventually, he would have come around. He would have seen his son fulfilling his heart's desire. I thought of you designing buildings that were to be built throughout the country—well, someone had to do it. Why could it not be my brother? I wanted you to follow your heart and your dreams.

"I want my son and my other children to grow up knowing you, but not from a distance. You have to be close enough to be able to get to know them and for them to know that they can rely on you.

"That is why you need to get this healing for your body. You have a future that waits for you, and you have to be ready. This is the time that you need to get ready."

I looked at her. I know that the astonishment was showing on my face. There were those words again! The same ones that I heard this morning while I was alone were just spoken to me by my sister. That was unbelievable; what were the odds of that happening?

I felt a hand on my shoulder and looked up to see Zeresh standing behind me. He spoke, "She is right, Gaius. This is the time that you need to get ready. There is something greater than you and any of us at work here. We cannot stand in the way, or we will get cut down like stalks of wheat that do not produce their bounty. You will have the strength when the time comes, but for now, you need to be ready for the work that is to be done within you."

I looked further behind him to where the rest of the men sat, totally silent as they waited to hear my decision. I did not understand the reason that they were all looking to me for an answer. I was not a ruler of this group. I realized that there were times when we had discussed things that needed to be done or places to which we should be traveling. But I felt that those decisions needed to be made by all of us. I was not trying to be someone who required others to follow whatever I said. Why now were they looking for me to make a decision that would affect the rest of our lives? They were all grown men and able to think on their own. They did not need me to give them instructions on how to live their lives.

Yet, deep inside of me, I knew that without me saying that together we were going, again, to make a trip to find Yeshua and ask for healing of our bodies, the decision was not going to be made. I sighed long and deep, lifting my hand to cover the hand of Zeresh that still lay on my shoulder and spoke loud enough so that everyone could hear, "We will go!"

The men stood to their feet; even Kalev did so on his own, lifting their hands and letting out such a long and loud shout I knew that my mother had heard it from the front yard in which she was standing. I could just see a smile coming to her face as she realized what had just occurred and walked back into the house, knowing the right decision had been made.

Moreda, forgetting that her shoes were off, stood up and started jumping up and down, clapping her hands, just as she had done when we were little. I was very much surprised that she would be able to do that at the age that she was then. But you know sisters—they always wind up doing the unimaginable!

I smiled at her as she quickly sat down to slip on her shoes before it registered in anyone else's mind that she was barefooted. Zeresh reached out and gave me a hug while the others around the table were slapping each other on the back and agreeing with one another that the next great adventure was about to begin for all of us.

The celebration continued even after Moreda left for home. She knew that she needed to be on the road to get back in order to help Mother prepare the evening meal. The word would be sent out to all the providers that the occupants of the camp were on their way to be healed, and only one last cooking of provisions would be needed. That would give us enough for the trip down to the border, and from there, we would rely on Adonai.

We all asked Moreda to let everyone know that we were all appreciative of the food, the time, and the thoughtfulness of everyone who had helped us in the past. She agreed that everyone in their circle of friends would hear that we were thankful for all their generosity.

This was about the time that Samuel and Keylie were bringing the water from the well for our daily needs. Moreda did not have to make the walk alone.

We went to our tents and began packing up our things for the trip that would begin the next day. It was as the sun was going down behind the mountains that we began our last night of resting in the camp of K'far-Nachum.

We were finally ready.

The trip to the countryside between Galil and Shomron had some unbelievable moments, but the excitement that we felt that evening at camp and the next morning as we prepared to leave continued to build in us every day. It was as if each and every one of us sensed that this was the time for which we had been waiting. The time that we had been hoping for so long would come our way. We stopped at midday to eat. Kalev was able to do a little more walking, most of the time that was in the morning when he was rested. After noon and the breaks that we took, we would help him along when he needed it.

We enjoyed seeing the countryside in bloom and the green grasses as they began to peek out from the ground. The trees were beginning to flower, and we would see farmers in the fields working with the crops that they had already planted. Lazerith told us that he had always wanted to be a farmer, to be able to help at his family's farm growing grains that would, in turn, be able to help feed families.

That led to a discussion around the group, and each of us took our turn to tell what we, as children, had thought about doing when we were all grown. Asha mentioned that he had always thought that he would be a teacher in the synagogue, as was his father and most of his family as far back as he could remember.

Manal and Elah said that they had always wanted to sail in the big boats that traveled from the country to some faraway land where they might meet other people or just work on boats that carried supplies to other lands. Who knows but what possibilities lie just over the horizon?

Hevel, Manulle, and David had always dreamed of being builders. They had been around carpentry at some point in their lives and had realized that it was a trade that they could pursue.

Zeresh and Kalev spoke that they had wanted to be soldiers, protecting those who could not protect themselves.

This subject alone took care of the conversations for about a week, and that took our minds off of why we were out walking the countryside.

We found a nice area close to a little town and a stream of water, where we set up camp for a few days. There were a couple of farms nearby that seemed happy to give up provisions. Then, we would hear about a group of people coming from the south. Thinking that it was Yeshua and His followers, we would break camp and head in that direction.

This went on for a couple of weeks. Then, our persistence paid off. We heard of people being healed a few towns over from where we were camping at that time. We didn't even take time to pack our things.

We immediately took off in that direction. As we neared a large crowd of people, I felt an excitement within me that I was unable to explain. By the looks on the faces of the men with which I had walked and camped for so many months, I could tell that they felt it too.

As we came closer to the village, I noted that it would be best not to go pushing through the crowd and hinted that maybe we stand on the side of the road closest to the hills. It would give us a distance from the road so as not to scare people but still near enough to be heard. Hevel posed the question that with the crowd talking among themselves, were we sure that when we spoke, we would still be heard?

Zeresh suggested that we call out in a loud voice as one. That should give us the ability to be heard over the crowd.

As Yeshua came closer, we, all together, called out, "Yeshua! Rabbi! Have pity on us!"

I was expecting Him to begin making His way to us as I remembered the story that Moreda had told me. When the healing of the man that was afflicted with tzara'at occurred, Yeshua had touched him. For so long, I had been waiting for that healing touch.

But we saw Him stop and look our way. He spoke these words to us, "Go and let the Cohanim examine you!"

Maybe if this had been a month or two before, I might have stopped and asked myself these questions: *Is that all it takes? We just had to go to the cohen and have him look at us, and we would have been cleansed? If we had known that, we could have gone to the temple long ago and asked a cohen to look at us so we could be healed.*

Maybe it was the way He said those words, the authoritative tone of His voice. All I know is that neither I nor anyone else in the group voiced the question of whether we should go or not. We did as we were directed. We all turned and walked up the road toward the town in order to find a cohen.

As we walked, Kalev mentioned that he was actually feeling the strength come back into his legs; he was able to move faster than he had in a few days. Zeresh noticed that the rashes on our faces and hands were growing lighter until they disappeared. I looked down at my own arms and saw the rash fade until it was gone.

I was amazed! How? Questions began flooding my mind, but also there were thoughts of thankfulness. I turned and began walking back in the direction from which we had just come. I had gone quite a distance before I realized that I was on my own. The others had continued walking toward town. They probably didn't even know that I was no longer with them.

As I got closer to where the group still stood around Yeshua, I began shouting praises to Adonai for the healing of my body for which I had waited so long. I fell down at the feet of Yeshua, thanking Him for ridding my body of the disease that had plagued me for these many years. I thanked Him for giving my life back to me. I would have continued to speak these words of thankfulness, but Yeshua spoke as He looked around,

"Were there not ten that were cleansed? Where are the other nine? Was no one found coming back to give glory to God except this foreigner?" To me, He spoke these words aloud, "Get up and go. Your faith has saved you."

He reached out a hand to help me to my feet. As I looked into His eyes, I heard Him say something,

"Gaius, you are now ready to begin the work that we have given you to do. You have had the strength to endure the pain of this terrible disease and the separation from your family. Therefore, I know that you will also have the strength that is needed for the days to come. You know how to help people, but sometimes, they just need you to be there to listen to them. Don't be too quick to want to fix things—to do things on your own. Simply explain what you would do in that circumstance and even give another way that might be helpful. Let others know that whatever decision they make will be up to them. You will be there when and if they ever feel that they need a friend.

"Do what is in your heart to do and enjoy your life, your family, and your friends. They will understand and will support you in what you set out to accomplish. You have been given this second chance. Now, go and do the same for someone else."

As He turned toward the crowd, I had the feeling that no one other than myself had heard those words. People were still talking and pressing forward to get a glimpse of this man of whom they had heard so much.

I wanted so much to stay with the crowd, to follow this man and learn from Him. But He had told me that I needed to go see a cohen. I began walking toward town, feeling better than I had in months. Strolling along as easily as I did when I was a young child, I continued to walk, alone and yet not alone. Never alone again!

The Cohanim declared that I was healed; they found no disease in my body. With that ringing in my ears and the joy still sounding in my heart, I began the walk back to K'far-Nachum and my family.

I walked as much as I could every day and well into the night as long as the light from the moon would shine on my path. I would rest for a while and then continue the journey. I would even join myself with a group or a single person who was walking in the same direction. It was nice to be close to people without them being afraid of me. I knew that I had to get back to show my mother and Moreda the miraculous cure that I had been given. I was whole once again.

One night, as I lay sleeping, I began a dream which seemed so familiar. I was on top of a hill, looking out over the landscape, just like the dream that I had before. Suddenly, I felt a difference in my dreaming.

It was as if instead of me being on a hill, I was on top of a mountain—many times higher than any mountain that I, in all my travels, could remember ever seeing. I could see more land, more rivers, lakes, and bigger bodies of water with more land on the other side. It seemed to me that I was no longer standing on the earth but on clouds far above it.

Straightaway, I felt a presence beside me and turned to see Gavri'el once again at my side.

"Fear not! I have brought another message for you. Now that you have been cleansed, you are ready to complete the work that Adonai has for you. Those who you have had in your life for so long have been waiting and watching to see the great change that is to be accomplished through you. Adonai will guide you in the paths that you will lead those who follow you. Great sacrifice has to come before great rewards. Many in your life have gone through the sacrifice that was needed in order for all to know the rewards that are now to be possessed."

As Gavri'el spoke, he gestured around the scene of the lands in front of me. I could see Manal and Elah on a boat sailing off to the west. Asha, to the south, was sitting with a group of young men as they listened to the figure that stood before them. I thought that this could be Yeshua, but as the man began walking around the room, I could tell that it was Peter. What was Peter doing teaching a group of men? He should be following Yeshua around the countryside!

As I began to wonder about the meaning of this sight, I felt a slight pressure on my shoulder and looked to see Gavri'el hand there. I knew that I had to stay with the vision that I was seeing and not get into my own thoughts and speculations. I brought my focus back to the surroundings that I saw.

Kalev and Zeresh were closer, and I could see that they were gathering a large group of men that looked to be going out to battle.

David, Hevel, and Manulle led a smaller band of men as they built houses and dwellings throughout the country.

Lazerith, I noticed, was hard at work in the farmlands that extended eastward.

I could feel the emotion rising in me, being proud of the men as they found happiness in those things which they had dreamed of doing for so long. I also knew that they would succeed in all that they would do in their careers and in their family lives. While continuing to survey the sights of these men, I knew what I needed to do. I believed that I had the ability to help ensure that all these things would happen.

The next morning, I awoke with a renewed knowledge of the things that I needed to do before focusing on myself and my future. Feeling refreshed and well-rested, I ate a bit of bread that had been left over from the previous day. Rising to my feet, I gathered my bundle and set out for home.

For the journey that had taken the group of ten two entire weeks to accomplish, I was able to make it back in four days.

As I walked down that path toward the house that had been so familiar from the outside, I realized that this would be the very first time that I would be welcomed inside my sister's home. I did not stop at the table and chair that had been set up for the outcast brother when the distance was needed. I walked right up to the door, calling out for Moreda as I did.

As she and Mother came in sight of the door, they both cried out in delight and gladness. I opened my arms and embraced them, holding them as they held me. I felt the tears flowing from their eyes as they dampened my clothing. I also felt tears streaming down my own face. I don't know how long we stood together holding each other. I do remember a little boy calling out for his mother. Moreda finally pulled away to see the boy. As she came back into the room, I noticed that she was not carrying him. I looked past her to see Micah walking through the doorway.

That glorious homecoming that I experienced lasted for days.

CHAPTER FOUR

A few days into my stay in Moreda's house, I awoke early and took a quick run toward the lake for my daily exercise. When I arrived back at the house, I found that there were visitors awaiting me. I entered the room and found David, Hevel, and Manulle, along with Zeresh and Kalev. After greeting the men with whom I had spent so much time over many months, I asked about the rest of our group. Zeresh told me that Asha had headed to Yerushalayim after our healing to begin his dream of becoming a teacher.

Upon hearing that, I sat down and wrote a letter to Asha. I told him that the rest of the men and I were glad that he was going to pursue his dream of being a teacher. We knew that he would become one of the best. I mentioned the dream that I had and asked him to wait in the area until he heard of a man called Peter. He was the one who would instruct Ashe in all the ways of teaching the people in the true ways of Adonai.

David and Zeresh set out for town to ask about any travelers that might be going down to Jerusalem. They were able to locate a group that was beginning the journey in a few hours, and one of the men agreed to stop at the house in order to pick up the letter that was to be delivered to Asha. We knew that he would be somewhere around the temple area and felt confident that the letter would reach him.

Manal and Elah were staying with friends in town and would be coming by for a visit in a few days. Lazerith had returned home to help his family with their farm, hoping that someday soon, he would have one of his own.

With so many men and a limited space in the house, we decided to set up a small camp out on the side of the house. It would almost be like being in our old camp, but it was entirely different and better since I was able to be close to my family. We spent many days speaking of getting on with the dreams of which we had spoken only a few weeks earlier as we traveled the roads.

When Manal and Elah arrived, I mentioned to them that my younger sister was married to a man who was in command of a ship. We could take a trip to visit them in Corinth and see if he had a place for them to become sailors if that was still something that they wanted to do with their future. They were in agreement that was what they wanted to do. Elah mentioned that his family had mentioned that they would be coming to the area to see him. His brothers had asked him to stay until they arrived as it had been such a long time since his parents had seen him.

Manal and Elah were going to remain in town with their friends and await the arrival of Elah's family along with my return. At that point, we would begin the trip to Corinth together for introductions to Jesse. While they were waiting for me, they planned to help their friends in any way that they were able.

After a month of getting reacquainted with my mother, sister, and her family, I announced that I was going to head to Sh'khem to see Giesell. I wanted to share with her the news of my cleansing. Also, I told Zeresh and Kalev we could go over to the Guard, and I could put in a good word for them to start their training.

A few days later, we six men began the trip to Sh'khem. While we traveled and rested, David, Hevel, Manulle, and I discussed going into our own business. While I could design buildings, they could use their carpentry skills to build them.

By the end of the week, we had arrived in town. Zeresh mentioned that we should go to the family home of Rivkah, knowing that we would be welcomed there. He was right!

The entire family came out in joyous celebration after recognizing Zeresh and learning of the healing that had been brought about in him. He introduced us all to them, and we had a wonderful time getting to know the family of which Zeresh had spoken so much. It warmed my heart to see that, throughout the trying times of the past years, the tzara'at disease that would take their daughter away from them, and the many months that Zeresh was gone away from the area, Rivkah's parents, Yitro (Jethro) and Elisheva (Elizabeth), still considered Zeresh to be part of their family. They also welcomed us as his friends. They allowed us to set up a camp in the field next to their house. We spent the night resting for the next morning's visit to the Guard.

I took Kalev and Zeresh out to the Guard's recruitment tent the next day. Some of the officers that we talked to seemed very familiar. When I told them who I was, they responded that I had been their training officer when they had started out in their careers. They thanked me for the leadership that I had given them. The conversation continued with engaging stories of how they had worked their way up in the ranks by using what I had taught them during those grueling training sessions.

After getting Kalev and Zeresh signed up and settled in their tents, we said our goodbyes and agreed that, somehow, we would keep in touch. I felt a large amount of sadness, knowing that it would be quite a while before I saw these two men in whose lives I had shared so much time.

I reminded Zeresh that he knew where Giesell's family home was and that I would be in town for at least a few more days. Even though I remembered that the first few days of training were rather long and strenuous, I made plans to come out and have a meal with them before leaving the area. They would also always be welcomed in K'far-Nachum, at Moreda's house. She and my mother would always know how they could get in touch with me, no matter where I might be.

Before I left, I asked Zeresh to stop in order to speak to him privately. Kalev had moved a few steps toward the tents, allowing us a few minutes. He realized since Zeresh had been with me since the very beginning of my illness, it was going to be more difficult to say our goodbyes.

I put my arm around him, hugging him tight and whispering in his ear, "Zeresh, I know that I have never told you this, but I forgive you." I pulled away from him a little so that I could look into his eyes.

"I never did put any blame on you for the disease that took over our lives. I know when you told me the story of how I had been the one who helped you after you were attacked, you said that it was all your fault. On that thought, I want you to know that I do not hold this bout of disease against you. I don't blame you at all. But if you blame yourself and cannot forgive yourself, I just wanted to say that I do forgive you.

"Even if you were the reason for the outbreak, I know, and you know, that it was all in the plans that Adonai had for us from the beginning of our lives. I don't know what I would have become if we had never met. I do know that watching you over these past months that we have been on this journey together, I have learned a lot from you.

"When you started spending more time in your relationship with Adonai, there was a great change in you. Many days, I would pray that He would make me more like you. You were so much more thoughtful and generous to the people around you while I was focused on myself and filled with bitterness. Sometimes, I thought that I actually hated the life that I had been forced to live.

"But every day, even when I was out traveling on my own, I knew that you had not given up on me. I realized that you and the petitions that you sent to Adonai were what kept me going toward the path that I needed to take in order to do all that was needed of me. I just wanted to say thank you, and even though I never had a brother, I want you to know that I will consider you my brother for the rest of our lives."

Zeresh reached a hand around my neck and pulled me to him in another hug.

"Gaius, I thank you for those kind words. I will forever be honored to be considered your brother." He broke away a bit and wiped tears from his eyes, then continued with more brotherly wisdom, "You have allowed Adonai to begin the work in your heart that will help you deal with whatever comes your way in future days. With the healing of our bodies from Yeshua, the healing of our spirits has also begun. That will be of great comfort and peace for what is about to come throughout this country and this region. I feel that there will be a great upheaval within our faith over the next few weeks. But Adonai has sent peace to my soul and has allowed me to know that all these things that will be happening will be for the good of all mankind.

"Please, keep yourself open for Adonai's leading in your life. I know that you will achieve everything that is needed of you."

With that, we embraced once more, and then he turned to join Kalev on the trip to the tent where they were to be staying.

At one point, as I walked down the road toward the main part of town, I stopped and looked back at the area that I had just left. Even though some of the tents appeared to be in good shape, there were many others that looked as if they had been there since the time when I had been in active service. Ragged edges, which had begun to show the thinness of the materials, were evident in many places.

I began to think that if the Guard was going to be in this area for longer than they had already been there, it might be a great idea to see if they would agree to have me design some buildings for them. Then, I could have David, Havel, and Manulle get the buildings into place for the recruits and the officers who needed to be housed at the camp. The men had spent enough time in tents, especially Zeresh and Kalev. It was time for them to have regular roofs over their heads.

By the time I had made it back to where we had been staying since our arrival in town, I was focused on getting something down on paper. I had stopped at a little shop where I found some parchment and writing tools that I could use. After eating our midday meal, I sat at the table and drew some sketches of what I thought would be practical for the men; places to sleep and separate places to eat or just gather and talk about things that were concerning to them. I showed different rooms that could be used for training talks and even an indoor training space so that, during the rainy season, they did not have to constantly be dredging through mud or puddles of water.

I then laid them in front of the others to get their opinions on whether these could be safely built. After hours of discussion, input from the others, and a few changes, we had plans for the whole facility that could change the face of the Guard for a very long time to come.

We had a small meal before the time came to rest for the day. I fell asleep thinking that tomorrow we could go back to camp, the four of us, and show the officers what we could actually do to help their cause. Once we had that lined up, I would actually be in a business that I thought might be able to support a family. Then, I would be able to meet with Giesell and see if she would agree to give our family another chance.

The next morning, we arrived at the camp and presented our plans to the officers. The new buildings would allow them to move out of the tents that now dotted the landscape. They were very open to the idea and made arrangements to meet with their supervisors to see if they could arrange for the funding needed to complete this project.

We walked back to town with much excitement, and within a few days, we received word that the Guard agreed to hire us to do the job. They even gave us an advance of the money to get the supplies that we were going to need.

David and Manulle had already been in contact with suppliers for the lumber, stones, and tools that were needed. Hevel had found a couple more men who had experience in carpentry and were willing to help with the construction. We also spent those extra days going over the plans for all the buildings, finding out which ones should be built first and the order that the remaining would be put up. I even spent more time making changes, seeing where some improvements might be made, and finally coming up to where I was satisfied with the plans that I had made.

The schedule was set. David, Hevel, and Manulle knew that they would share in overseeing all the construction and had promised me that they would bring honor to all the work that I had put into the designing of these buildings.

Within a few days, the five men arrived at the camp, and the work began. I saw them leave that morning and asked Adonai to watch over them, to give them the skill to accomplish what we were setting out to do at the camp, and for Him to give me the words to speak when I went over to talk to Giesell. I waited for an hour or two before beginning the walk to her house. I was not sure what I would find, whether she was still there or had decided to move on with her life. It had been quite a long time since I had left her there after she had decided to stay with her family. I took the walk very slowly, trying to arrange in my mind the words that I would speak to her while imagining what her response would be to all that I had to say.

Upon arrival, I walked into the yard and toward the door. A couple of children came running around from the side of the house and noticed me standing there. One of them ran into the house to announce that there was some man coming to visit. A woman, whom I took as Caleb's wife, came out and asked why I was there. I told her that I would like to speak to Giesell. She turned and called out, asking me to wait, and then returned to the house. Within a few minutes, I saw Giesell coming out the door.

As she got in sight and could tell it was me, with a look of surprise on her face, she began to run. I opened my arms and gathered her up as tightly as possible. She held on to me for what seemed to be hours, tears streaming down both of our faces. She was able to whisper in my ear, "Yeshua?" All I could do was nod my head against hers in acknowledgment.

We finally calmed down enough for her to invite me into the house, and we sat talking for the remainder of the day. She asked how things had happened, how Mother and Moreda were doing, and what plans I had. She also inquired about the other men in the group, and I mentioned that all were cleansed as I was by Yeshua. There were so many questions on both our parts that, at one time, we looked at each other and began laughing. I told her that there would be plenty of time for us to find out all these things together if she thought that we could be a family again.

A slight cloud came over her face, and the smile left her lips. She looked at me without speaking for a moment. Reaching over to take my hand in hers, then looking down to her lap, she began, "Gaius, do you think that is the wisest thing for you to do? I mean, with all that I did after leaving you, how can you believe that me being your wife would bring you anything but pain and shame?"

I squeezed the hand that I held and, with the other hand, raised her chin so I could look into her eyes. "Giesell, one of the things that I have learned through the happenings of the many months gone by is that everyone deserves a second chance. I am not a perfect individual. There is not a single human on earth that is perfect. We are all mistake-ridden throughout the time that we have been given. But by our stumbling, we learn, and when we find ourselves in that situation again, we can choose a better path to take.

"This world around us and the people who are in authority have messed up our minds and thoughts by putting ideas and desires before us, things that they want us to believe are the best for us. And they don't want us to question anything that they tell us. Many people follow those authorities blindly, believing all that they are being told is true.

"Then, there are other leaders who are so far off the path with what they believe that sometimes it scares me to think of what these people are capable of doing to others around them. It shocks me to know that they are also telling people what they consider to be the truth that everyone should follow, that all they do is for the betterment of the people.

"When we are young and inexperienced, our parents are the ones who make decisions of what they think is right for us because we do not know any better way. Having lived through similar circumstances, we look to them for guidance, knowing that, as our parents, they would never steer us wrong. They would want to keep us from all the things that they might have undergone in their past, to save us from any hurt that they might have gone through. That is why it is important to listen to our elders.

"But as we grow into adulthood, it becomes our responsibility to do the decision-making for ourselves. People might give us their opinions or might tell us what they would do if they were in the same position. Ultimately, it is up to each individual to decide for themselves, and what might be right for one person might not be what is right for another. Adonai gave us all minds of our own and the ability to make decisions that are needed in our lives. He also gave us guidelines to follow in order to keep us on the right path.

"We need to remember that things just don't end with the choices that we make; we have to live with the consequences of those selections. We are in control of what we do. We do not have the right to blame others for how our lives turned out.

"We might have someone in our lives who we are very close to; it could be one of our family members. And they have made a decision in their life that may have put us in a particular situation where we find ourselves having to deal with some abnormality in our life. But we cannot know whether the decision that person made was or was not the correct one for them. We just know that it affected us in a way that we were not expecting.

"The outcome for all things lies in the options of what we decide is right for us. But also, we can make changes in what we do in this day and in the future. We get to the point where we learn from all the mistakes that we have made in the past. We cannot alter any of what we have done, yet we can learn how to be better at living now.

"I see that is what occurred in my life when I was younger and thought about designing buildings while Abba wanted me to follow in his footsteps and live my life in the military. Up to a point, I knew that I had in front of me two paths that would lead to the decisions that would take me down the road, which would decide the direction of my life.

"The first path showed me as going ahead with the dreams that I had, which might have led me to great fame—being known as a designer of buildings that could have given me a name that would be recognized by people all over the country. There was also a chance that it would be a disaster. It might have brought me to the point where I was laughed at by all that saw my designs. I had no training to help me accomplish any of the tasks that I might face in order to fulfill the dreams that I had. I had to decide if I wanted to take the chance of that happening to my family.

"The second path was the one where I could see Abba's footsteps because that is the path that he had taken. Those footsteps looked familiar and safe, so that is the way that I began my life's journey."

I paused for a moment when I saw the look of astonishment on Giesell's face. I recognized that look and realized that I had been talking for a considerable amount of time. (I guess that it could be said that I had spent too much time with Moreda—her ability to go on and on for hours seemed to have rubbed off on me.) Yet, I knew that there were other things that I needed to say to her. I rose to my feet, and while holding her hand, I helped her to stand beside me. We walked out the door into the yard, and I motioned to that tree that stood near the path, the one that I had seen a few months ago.

"I think of our lives as like the branches on that tree. When we started out, we were the trunk coming out of the ground. We can start out on the left side or the right side; that really doesn't matter. With every decision that we make, we branch out from that point of our beginning. The small twigs that grow from the branches represent the choices that we had to make but didn't follow through to completion. They can also represent people who have come into your life. Then, we continue, as the branch, to grow and follow the paths that take us throughout our lives.

"When you were growing up, you saw for yourself how your father was treated as a member of the council. You thought that was the best life there was because it was so much better than those families that you saw around you. You were invited to festivities and celebrations that many of us never knew existed. Of course, we had our family gatherings and our holy days, but they were never to the extent of the shows that you observed while you were a child.

"As you grew older, you wanted that all to continue. You felt that you deserved all that and more because you were familiar with that type of life. You believed what you saw and what you heard was the best life that you could have desired. It was what you had been taught, whether on purpose or by mere coincidence, and that was all that you knew. That is why you pursued it, and it was not your fault.

"During the time that we were together, you were able to see a life that was very different from how you were raised. You were beginning to see how life was for most people in our town and in many countries. That life was interrupted by the tzara'at that took over my body which in turn changed our lives. You were scared to think that something as small as a rash on my neck should have brought about so much change in our lives.

"I believe that what you realized was that when you were in your earlier life, at home with your family, you did not have to deal with anything like this disease. The place that you had lived in was solid and predictable; you thought that you would be safer if you were still in that life. And that is why, I believe, you tried your hardest to return to it. A time when things were simpler and happier and when you did not have to deal with real life. But you found that the change had already begun in you. No matter how hard you tried, you could not get back to those carefree, innocent days for which you were longing."

"Gaius, you are right. I realized that no matter how much I wanted to do so, I could not go back in time to my life as it had been. And all the things that I remembered from my younger years were just in the mind of a child. What really went on—even back then, was kept from us by our parents.

"If I had been in my parent's positions, I would have seen the same things that I witnessed in these past years. I mean, as a child, you are kept away from all the conversations and all the insults that are spoken by adults. As an adult, I heard all those slights, all those put-downs by others that I thought were friends. But they were just playing a part, acting as other people had told them to act.

"Still, to live here and have people around us that remember what I was doing, how I was living…."

That is where I stopped her. "We don't have to live here. There is a whole world out there—many other towns and cities from which we can choose to live."

"But you have your friends building the quarters for the Guard. You will have to stay in order to see that your job is completed."

I smiled and grasped her hand more tightly. "I don't have to stay. My job here is completed. I only design the buildings. David, Hevel, and Manulle, along with their crews, are the ones that are doing the building. They are the ones that will remain here until the work is completed. And I have left this job in very capable hands. I know that they will do the best that they can. Plus, we can travel back here to see it when all is done.

"We are now able to begin our new life together, to do that traveling that we had spoken about all that time ago. We can start a whole new adventure of our own."

Later that evening, I asked Giesell if she would marry me again. She agreed, and within a few days, we had a small ceremony with her family and our closest friends that were in the area. Dorlas was there, beaming with pride and letting everyone know that she was the one who had taken care of us when we could not care for ourselves.

David, Zeresh, Manulle, and I were treated to big hugs from her, and we expressed our thankfulness once again for her willingness to come out to the camp and care for strangers. She even gave Kalev a hug after knowing him for that brief time when we had come back to town. Her love and care made us all feel like we were family.

We stayed for an extra week while the building of the Guard facilities continued. After being told by David and Hevel that they had all things under control and Manulle having hired more workers to get the job completed before too much longer, Giesell and I embarked on a trip around the countryside as we made our way back to Capernaum.

Yes, I said Capernaum.

Before we left, David sat down with me one evening after dinner and spoke to me about changing some things in my own life. He knew how much my Jewish heritage had played a big role in my upbringing, and while some older people of our faith still used the words that were so familiar to us, it was time for me to move into the real world in which we would be working and living. I had to learn how to speak to people in a way that they could understand me. I agreed with him; therefore, I began to assimilate a new language into my life. I would never have thought that in those later years of my life, I would have to learn a second language!

The trip that took Giesell and me from Sychar to Capernaum lasted a few weeks. That time was spent getting to know each other again. I showed her some of the places through which I had traveled, and she was astonished by many things that were new to her.

We arrived at Moreda and Peter's house early one morning. The homecoming celebration that we received there was like no other. Moreda had another child to take care of while Micah was growing so fast. I hardly recognized him as being the same little boy that I remember leaving just a short time ago.

Mother was still herself, going strong, helping throughout the neighborhoods of the town wherever she was needed. They had wanted another ceremony so that they could witness and bless the reuniting of Giesell and me as a family. Upon hearing this request, Giesell smiled at me as we both remembered on the return trip, I had stated that my family would want a ceremony to witness that we were indeed a couple again. We agreed to a small one.

Upon our return, I had sent word to Elah and Manal that we were back in town, and if they were still wanting an introduction to Jesse and a life in the sailing business, we needed to get them on their way to fulfilling their dreams. Before the end of the month, the four of us set out on the trip to Corinth.

Prior to leaving, I had received word from David that the Guard's buildings were in the finishing stages, and by the time we arrived back in Capernaum, they would be completed, and we could find the next job that needed to be done.

Traveling by foot, we made it to Tyre and found passage on

a boat that was sailing to Crete. From there, after a few days, we were able to find a ship that would take us to Greece.

Giesell had a rough couple of days as this was the first time that she had ever been on a boat, but after that, she enjoyed the trip greatly. She would stand at the railing and let the wind blow through her hair. With a smile on her lips, she would watch the fish and the other sea creatures gliding through the waters.

Arriving in Corinth, we located Jesse and Delai's house. I was shocked when I first saw my younger sister but realized that we had been apart for so many years that changes were inevitable. She was now grown up, a wife and mother of three girls. We sat and spoke for hours while awaiting Jesse's return to port. Delai and Giesell became close friends.

Elah and Manal took to walking the docks, finding small jobs here and there during the time of waiting. I even began walking around the city, noticing the buildings that were standing and making notes of things that I would like to merge with other ideas that I had in mind. By the time Jesse arrived back home, I had quite a few pages of designs ready to be built.

Jesse agreed that Elah and Manal would be great workers for his ships. Within days, they were on board, training for their life on the open sea.

Giesell and I stayed on for another few weeks enjoying the time that we had with family. During that time, travelers were coming through from our region, and word was spreading fast about a great teacher being killed by Roman soldiers. The details that had been brought in were few since it was a message from one passed on to another—you know, portions of the information seem to get lost or misspoken. We figured we would hear the true story when we arrived back home.

Soon, we began our travels back to Capernaum and new beginnings.

By the time we arrived back, we had found out that the young teacher, Yeshua, had been the one who had been put to death. It was a strange story, filled with dread and sadness. Yet, while sitting down with Mother and Moreda, listening to them speak to us about the time following the death, their take on things was very different.

According to the things that they had heard from Peter, after three days, Yeshua was alive and walking the roads with other men.

Peter had even come back into town and began to go out on the fishing boats again. Then, he saw Yeshua and left the boats, never to return to that life again. Yes, he did come home to visit with his family, but like Yeshua, he was soon gone again. He went around the countryside and into Jerusalem, teaching the news of Yeshua, who was the Son of God.

I was skeptical about all this resurrection from the grave bit of the story. I mean, how can a person who is dead return to life? Once you're gone, you are gone; there's no coming back, right? It didn't seem possible to me.

Giesell and I would see Peter from time to time, and whenever I did, I would remember the man at whose feet I fell, thanking Him for the second chance at life that He had given to me. After the many months that I was an outcast, shunned by most of the people who would walk the same roads as me, there was hope, at last, for something different. I was given a new life.

One of these times, when we were able to meet with Peter, I sat down to talk to him about the very subject of resurrection. I told him that I wanted to believe the story, but people coming back from the dead isn't something that you hear of very often.

He sat there before me, and his countenance was so much different than what I believe I ever saw. I recalled the first time that I saw him—that time after Abba died. He and Moreda had come to town to get Mother moved in with them. Peering through the cloth that covered my face, I remember a joyful light in his eye, a happiness that I took to mean that he and Moreda were enjoying their life together. After getting to know him, I could see that he and Moreda found comfort in their union.

Now, there was definitely contentment in his manner that made me believe that he knew the secrets of life. He explained that throughout the time that he had spent as one of the disciples of Yeshua, he was witness to many of the miracles that He performed on the weakest and the helpless of people. He had indeed known of a girl that was brought back to life and of a widow's son that was raised as the funeral procession was going down to the grave site. And just a few days before the final trip to Jerusalem, Yeshua raised a dear friend that had been dead and buried in the grave for four days.

Then, Peter spoke to me the words that Yeshua had spoken on that day, "I am the resurrection and the life. The one who believes in Me will live, even though they die, and whoever lives by believing in Me will never die."

It took me a while to understand what Peter had told me that day. Sometimes, I wished that I had had more time to spend with Peter, Yeshua, and the group who traveled with Him. I believe that I would have learned so much more if I had the firsthand knowledge that Peter and the others had received.

There are so many things that I am not sure of, but that does not mean that my mind is closed to anyone or anything that is different from what I have been taught in the past. I still remember that our people were promised a Redeemer, the Messiah, who would come to free people who were enslaved.

And in a way, I believe that Yeshua was the Messiah, as others had said long before His death. After all, wasn't it He that had freed me, Zeresh, and the rest of our group that suffered from leprosy? He had freed blind ones from darkness; He had freed the lame from having to rely on people to carry them around from place to place. He had freed many sick people from whatever disease or sickness had held their bodies or minds. He had freed those of us who believed that we were nobodies, that we didn't count as human beings. We do belong in this life. We were put on this earth with a purpose; there is something that we are to accomplish. It is up to us to find out what it is and then do it. And I believe that Yeshua was able to show many people that they, too, have a purpose in life. He taught them the way to be more like Him.

Truthfully, I believe that we need more people in this world who are willing to be more like Him. The person who He really was—not just someone's perspective of what He was like. Someone who was willing to go beyond the normal duties of this life and let strangers know that they do matter, that they are worthy of a smile and a kind word. And from that time on, I tried to be more like that man who had given me my second chance in life.

****

Giesell and I would begin a family, living just down the road from Mother and Moreda. We enjoyed our life together and always remembered that Adonai was always present. We had a lot of years together and enjoyed every one of them.

I would go on to build a great business with the help of the crews that actually did the construction of many structures that dotted the countryside throughout Galilee, Samaria, and Judah.

David, Hevel, and Manulle, along with their constantly expanding crews, labored diligently on the projects that were requested by many who had heard of the great work that was being done around the area. Within a few years, we were the best-known builders in all of Galilee.

The men also found wives who were willing to be uprooted many times in order for them to continue the business. Then, when the families were beginning to expand, David suggested that they train the younger men on the crews to do the traveling and oversee the builders.

With Hevel and Manulle, it took a few more years before they began to slow down, but with age taking its toll on all of us, we knew when it was time to let others do the heavy lifting. We knew when it was time to rest.

Mother was the first to leave us, after fifty years on this earth and being able to share so much wisdom in those years we had her with us. I know that she was proud of what she had accomplished in the life that she had been given. As I think about my sisters and the families that they raised, I know that they are continuing the teachings that they have learned.

After Mother died, Moreda and the children began to travel with Peter. Not all over the country, but when he was in a certain city, they would meet up with him, traveling to a couple of different towns and spending time together as a family while they could do so. It was not a life that I would have wanted my sister to have, but she was happy. She loved Peter, understood that what he was doing was the right thing, and knew that he was the one who needed to do it.

A few years after that time, she arrived back in Capernaum and mentioned that Peter had been killed. His life had been taken because of his teachings and the faith that he had in God.

They had all been in Corinth at the time. Moreda and the children were spending time with Delai and her family. Peter would join them in the evenings and would be off the next morning to continue teaching the people of Yeshua.

Then, one late afternoon, one of the men that followed Peter came to the house and relayed the news of Peter's death. After that, more news came of other believers of Yeshua being put to death because of their beliefs.

I didn't understand why this thing had happened. Why would anyone be killed because of their beliefs? Was it now against the laws of man for people to believe in different things?

If I were to say to someone that I believe that the sun is what gives life to the grass of the field, would I be killed because of what I believed? If I thought that rain which muddied our roads and pathways so badly that we could not walk, was punishment for things that we did, would my life be taken from me because of that belief?

It took me a while to make sense of the happenings around us. But then it occurred to me. Peter was not killed for what he believed, he was killed because he was telling others of the teachings of Yeshua, and people around the country, in turn, were beginning to believe.

If more people heard and continued to believe, this would not bode well for the Roman emperor or for anyone who was trying to rule the people. It would not take long for an uprising to occur, and no one in power wanted a revolt against their governing authorities. Yet, I knew deep down inside me that the uprising would happen sometime in the future. I did not know if I would be around when it did, but *it was coming*! I could feel it.

Also, after hearing more about the teachings of Peter and

understanding other men in their group who had the privilege of knowing and hearing Yeshua, I was positive that many changes were on the horizon.

These were the teachings that would take the people away from the beliefs and laws placed on our people by the leaders of the synagogue.

I am reminded of another time that I had a chance to hear Peter talking about another message that Yeshua had spoken. It was before a great multitude of people when these words were spoken.

"You have heard that our fathers were told, 'Eye for eye and tooth for tooth.' But I tell you not to stand up against someone who does you wrong. And, you have heard that our fathers were told, 'Love your neighbor—and hate your enemy.' But I tell you, love your enemies! Pray for those who persecute you! Then, you will become children of your Father in heaven. For He makes His sun shine on the good and bad people alike. Therefore, be perfect, just as your Father in heaven is perfect."

Now, if we, the people, would begin believing these words, how much authority would the Pharisees still have over us? We as a people would be changing our beliefs, and *change* is what the leaders fear most!

Sadly, Giesell left me too soon, yet different from the other times, I knew that she would always be with me. I could see her in the faces of our daughters and in the eyes of our sons. I thank Adonai every day for giving me the life that I had, even though times were strange for a while. I constantly found that I had the strength inside of me to help me through it all.

If I were able to go back to the very beginning, I don't think that I would change a single thing. Early in my time as a leper, there were moments when I thought I would have made changes if possible. I could have had a continuously good life with Giesell; we would have started a family while we were younger. Abba and Mother would have been able to be together for a long period of time and enjoyed more of their grandchildren.

But if I hadn't contracted leprosy, would I have even met David or Kalev or even remembered the encounter with Zeresh? Maybe his life would have been saved by some other traveler instead of me. Would I have continued in my military career and become one of the high-ranking officials or maybe even died in battle? One thing that I do know for sure—if I had never become a leper, Giesell would have never been the woman that met Yeshua at the well.

There were always different outcomes of my life that would play out in my head when I got to play the "What If?" game.

Yet, I know in my soul that the circumstances that I faced throughout my life were what was required to happen in order to get me to the place where I needed to be. All the things that I was able to accomplish, and the friendships that I had made, which continued to grow stronger throughout the years, that is what I had been placed on this earth to do.

If I had tried to change even one thing that had occurred in my younger years, I am sure that it would have begun an apocalyptic event from which I would never be able to recover. I am just thankful that I had the right amount of wisdom passed down from my parents and all the people that I met along the way who had directed my life decisions.

No, I didn't need to have a great career in the Guard. I didn't need a medal given to me. I didn't need a statue built in my honor. All I needed to accomplish I did without fanfare or any great celebration. And that's the way that it was meant to be. I may have gotten side-tracked a couple of times, but eventually, I got back on the path that would take me throughout my journey on this earth.

At this point in my writing of these words, I don't know how much longer I have left on this earth. It could be another four years or only four days. But as I look back on my life and all it entails, I am amazed that I have lived this long. All of the ups and downs, the traveling that I did while alone and later in life with the men of the camp, and later still, the travels that Giesell and I took together were all exciting. Even during the time that I was infected with leprosy, I was able to learn many things. I grew into the man that I needed to be, and I am happy with what I have accomplished. I am glad that Adonai gave me the strength that I needed and helped me through all those bleak times.

When it is time for me to take that last walk down the lane or sit beside my children, listening to their children playing in the yard or enjoying a holy day with the family, I will just say that it was all well worth the voyage.

And what a voyage it was!

CONCLUSION

Coming through all of this at the age that I sit here now, writing out the words, thoughts, feelings, and the story of my life, I wonder what should be the words that I leave with you so that you will know what I needed to tell you through my story.

There are some things that I left out intentionally, such as all the pain and suffering that a person with leprosy goes through over the course of the disease. Many things I could have gone to great lengths to explain, but I thought it would be best if you did not know my fellow sufferers or me through those eyes. Let me just say that I am glad that you are not one who has to go through it all.

On to the things that I do want to tell you, one thing is: Don't be afraid of things that you don't understand. Most of us are not born smart. We don't know how the world works, but as we grow and learn how things work around us, we find out exactly what we need to do in order to not only survive but to live the life that we have been given.

Study the people around you. Learn about others and learn from others. There might be someone in your town that was not raised as you have been. They might have even come from a different country, a different culture. But they are living in your town now. It is a place that they call home, just as you do. Therefore, don't keep believing that they are outsiders. They want to be a part of the community, and you need to welcome them as a member of it.

Don't let *anyone* take your dreams away from you. Whatever you want to do, whatever you set your mind to do, do all that you can to accomplish that goal.

It might take a lot of education, so study what you need to learn and all that is required to succeed.

It might take a lot of strength, but you have inside of you what is needed to achieve your dream.

It might take a lot of hard work. Put your mind to it and persevere even when you face opposition or discouragement.

Your dreams might come soon, or it might take a lot more time than you thought. Don't get sidetracked. Keep focused on your ambition, and it will come to pass.

Don't be afraid to ask for help. We all have the strength that is given to us, but sometimes, we just need more than what we have. You should have others in your life who will love you, not just people who are mere acquaintances. People close to you who will be willing to help if only they know that you need it. Let them know when you are struggling, for they will come to assist you in every way possible.

But you also need to remember that it goes both ways—the help might flow into you when you are in great need of it. Yet, your friends and your family need to know that when they are the ones who are lonely or troubled about something in their lives, they can count on you to be there for them. Even if they just need to talk, be there to listen. Don't think that you need to fix everything or mention something that you are experiencing. Remember that this time it is not about you. Don't speak; just listen.

Learn to live in the moment. Do not focus on the past, as there is nothing that you can do to change it. You can learn from it, however. If you have gone through a rough time at an earlier point in your life, do not neglect to acknowledge that in your later life. You might be going through a stormy time that is similar to what you experienced earlier. You can take what you learned throughout your years and may come up with a better way of handling things.

Rely on wisdom from your elders as they have been living on this earth longer than you have. They have seen things in their life that are totally different from what you have witnessed. But just because it is different, don't believe that you cannot learn from what they are saying. They will probably have insight on a lot of things that you would never have considered possible. The circumstances might be unlike the ones that you find yourself in at that particular time, but using the wisdom that they share with you might get you to the same conclusion.

Do not fear the future because no matter what comes, you will be able to handle it, even if you don't believe that you can. The strength lies within you.

Enjoy the time that you have been given. Enjoy the people that have been placed in your life. Because, like you, they were put here for a reason. *You* might just be the one whom they need to discover what that reason is. Be willing to spend time with them and impart knowledge that might help them in becoming aware of what that purpose might be for them.

Most of all, remember that everyone deserves a second chance. I got mine. You got one, too, didn't you? Can you actually imagine that we are the only ones who are entitled to the grace of being allowed that chance? No! We are not any better than anyone else. When I say that everyone deserves a second chance: I mean *everyone!* What each individual does with that second chance is up to them and their conscience; they will have to live with the choices that they make, just as you will, just as I did.

I guess that is all I have to say. I hope that I have not rambled on about too much. You know how it is with old folks! We tend to think that every little detail has to be spoken to everyone, so they will understand all that we know.

Genna has come into the room with a request for her grandfather. She wants me to meet a man that she met a few weeks ago. He would like to speak with me. About what? I don't know. But she seems to think that this man will make a difference in our world. I guess that we will see about that. Or maybe I should say that you will see about that. I don't think that I will be around for another adventurous journey on this earth.

I do have one last question: *Who* in the world is Flavius Josephus?

****

AUTHOR'S NOTE

Upon mentioning this last statement to someone close to me, the point was made that people may not know of Josephus, of whom it was mentioned. There are those, in this day and time, that might think that this is a lead-in to a sequel—it is not.

Flavius Josephus was a first-century Romano-Jewish historian. Josephus recorded Jewish history. His most important works were *The Jewish War* and *Antiquities of the Jews*.

The Jewish War recounts the Jewish revolt against Roman occupation.

Antiquities of the Jews recounts the history of the world from a Jewish perspective for Greek and Roman readers. These works provide insight into first-century Judaism and the background of early Christianity.

While there is no record that Josephus ever met and talked with a man named Gaius, there is also no record that he did not meet with such a man.

CPSIA information can be obtained
at www.ICGtesting.com
Printed in the USA
BVHW051948050423
661819BV00010B/181

9 798887 386737